# 7 MINUTES TO WIN IT!

*Impact, ignite* and *inspire* your audience
in just **7 minutes** of speaking!

# MALACHI TALABI

Cover picture credit:
Adebayo Deru of Creative Piece – www.creativepiece.com

Design and layout:
Kaye Homecillo

Published by MTalabi Enterprise

# DEDICATION

I dedicate this book to you.

You may have picked up this book because you're looking to grow as a speaker so you can make an impact in the world and leave an impression on someone's heart.

Or maybe you just want to be better at giving a 7 minute speech at your Toastmasters club or contest.

Whatever your reason may be, I hope that *7 Minutes to Win It* will help you to construct and deliver a good speech so that you can impact, ignite and inspire your audience each and every time you speak.

I wish you the very best.

# CONTENTS

# ABOUT THE AUTHOR

In July 2010 Malachi joined the world-renowned Toastmasters International public speaking and leadership programme and made an immediate impact by winning the Humorous Speech public speaking competition at club and south London area level within three months of joining.

Just six months later in May 2011, Malachi became the UK and Ireland public speaking champion and then went on to Las Vegas in August 2011 to compete in the world finals where he placed third in the semi-final rounds, a feat no other British person had achieved in three years.

---

*"I saw Malachi deliver his winning speech at the District 71 International Speech Contest and knew he was something special. When I was planning the first ever Toastmasters Division J event for people across the South West corner of the UK, I knew that it was vital that they were inspired and got to experience what 'outstanding' looked like. I was delighted when Malachi came to see us and shared 'the truth behind the trophy' and he did a great job. He was funny, personal and inspirational all at the same time and the audience were gripped. A number of people spoke to me afterwards and said how much they had enjoyed and valued his speech. For me personally, it was a salutary reminder to get outside my comfort zone – in short, he was a great success!"*

**Jean Gamester**

**(Division J Governor – Toastmasters International, District 71)**

Malachi speaks professionally at events and conferences and delivers public speaking workshops on topics including: "The secrets of successful public speaking", "How to connect with your audience in an instant", and "Public speaking: from good to great".

Malachi is also the author of three books, a speech coach and a passionate football player and fan.

To book Malachi for a keynote, workshop, or for a coaching session, email hello@malachitalabi.com or go to www.malachitalabi.com.

# ACKNOWLEDGEMENTS

My journey from Bermondsey to Las Vegas in 2011 would not have been possible without some very generous individuals who helped me along the way.

I would like to thank Jim Key for his amazing coaching and support before and in Vegas; Phillip Khan-Panni for helping me to improve my speech Keep on Walking and my speaking as a whole; and Simon Bucknall for graciously lending me his entire set of Toastmasters contest winning DVDs which were a great help to me when preparing for the semi-finals.

I'm also grateful to my first Toastmasters club, Croydon Communicators, especially David Thompson, Hanna Hunter, Dave Longley, Vathani Navasothy, Peter Gerlach and Philip Landergan – your support has been amazing.

There are so many other wonderful people in District 71 who supported me in some way including Dave Selman, Samantha Babister (you planted the seed, thank you), Teresa Dukes, Freddie Daniels, Iain Duthie, Rory Marriott, Hilary Briggs, Bob Nisbet, Aaron Wood, Richard Murray, Gordon Piggott, Jim Hegarty and Julie Kertesz.

Karen and Len Allen – thank you for cheering me on at Windsor and your constant support. I can't wait until Amario takes the stage!

I would also like to thank Maureen Burns Zappala, Scott Pritchard, Lisa Panarello, Omar Rivas, Granard McClendon, Arnita Jones, Phil Barth and Dhanashree Thangaraja for their generous contributions to this book.

And thank you to two more champions — my first editor Karen Dods for unscrambling my thoughts and asking me challenging questions about the manuscript; and my precious wife Mildred for adding the crucial finishing touches to the editing process and for being patient and loving enough to hear me practice a thousand times, evaluate me, and still smile when my 7 minutes are over — you are a star!

# FOREWORD

In today's world, being able to communicate effectively and efficiently is critical to success. If you know that someone had expertise and experience from which you could benefit, and that person stood ready to assist you, would you be excited about receiving that assistance? That is what this book represents.

When I met Malachi Talabi in May 2011, it was clear to me that he was both an effective and efficient communicator. It was in Windsor, UK at the UK & Ireland 2011 Public Speaking Championships. Several years prior I achieved the title of World Champion of Public Speaking by winning a series of contests that culminate in a worldwide championship — hence the title. Malachi was vying to become one of my successors; he was involved in one of the rounds of speech contests which are part of the World Championships. I watched him speak for a mere 7 minutes, but I witnessed him deliver a highly effective message that impacted that audience long beyond the time he spoke.

After Malachi won that particular contest, I got the chance to work with him as he prepared for the subsequent rounds of the speech contest series. I found him to be very impressive, both in the manner in which he assimilated input and advice and weighed it against how it might serve his purpose, and in the way he never lost track of his own speaking style during the process. It was obvious that he was a great student but also someone with a strong sense of who he is and his personal communication style.

That Malachi's accomplishments are impressive are an understatement. Reading this book made clear to me that he has made the transition from student to instructor, and is willing to share the things he has learned during his journey for the benefit of his readers — THAT is both a joy and a privilege for me to witness.

Irish playwright, George Bernard Shaw, is quoted as saying:

*"The single biggest problem in communication is the illusion that it has taken place."*

Malachi isn't just a speaker. He is a communicator who knows how to get past that illusion and to make sure that effective communication does take place – his awards are evidence of that. But that is only part of the story. Not content to simply be an expert communicator, Malachi has penned this book to share the tips and techniques and secrets and strategies he learned which will enable you to become the same – a communicator who is highly effective, especially when you have a short amount of time in which to convey your message.

As you read this book, you will identify practical things you can do to improve your effectiveness as a speaker. As you begin to put into practice what you learn, your skills as a speaker will grow. Your reputation as a master communicator will grow. More importantly, the benefit experienced by your audiences . . . will grow.

Just be sure to send Malachi a 'thank you' note when that occurs! ☺

**Jim Key**
**2003 World Champion of Public Speaking**

# PREFACE

Out of 25,000 contestants from all around the world, I placed in the top 30 in a Toastmasters International Speech Contest held in Las Vegas in August 2011.

I had only been a Toastmaster for nine months. I was new to speaking: my mum wasn't a professional speaker; neither was my dad. I just joined Toastmasters because my wife suggested it. In fact, I wasn't even really interested in speaking! It was so overwhelming I didn't even intend to enter competitions! But three months into my Toastmasters journey, I won two humorous speech contests, and reached the World Semi-finals of the International Speech Contest six months later, after winning several previous rounds.

Round after round, I attributed my wins to luck. I thought God was on my side – well, that was true, but this was more than heavenly intervention. I began to realise that I wasn't just naturally gifted and favoured, this was systematic. Round by round, I was learning and applying patterns, rules, skills and tools that helped me shape my speech and win.

Who would have known that I, Malachi Talabi, would be called an award-winning speaker? At times, it's still a shock to me! I am a footballer, I enjoy singing, and I currently work as a teaching assistant. Public speaking, let alone award-winning public speaking, wasn't on the agenda at all. Winning the contest on my very first try was the furthest thing from my mind!

As I journeyed through the contest circuit, I had to face two facts: 1) I was a young speaker; 2) I was inexperienced. These facts now help me share the simple truth that you can enhance your speaking skills with a little time and the right tools.

I have had my season on the stage: I loved the contest environment. I loved the opportunities that winning has given to me and the wealth of knowledge I have picked up on my journey. As you read this book, get ready to **impact, ignite** and **inspire** your audience each time you speak.

May this be your new mantra:

**"Give me 7 seconds and I'll tell you a joke; give me 7 minutes and I will touch your life . . ."**

# INTRODUCTION

Imagine being handed a ticket to Las Vegas to speak with some of the best speakers in the world in front of hundreds of people, all because of one speech you gave?

Imagine standing on a stage and watching as your words penetrate the surface and reach deep into the souls of your audience? Imagine being told a speech you gave helped someone through a devastating situation?

Now imagine doing that in just 7 minutes!

I am still amazed that a 7 minute speech could have that much impact on my life and the life of my audience members, but it did. And your speech can have that impact on your audience as well, whether you are giving a short business presentation, addressing a university, or competing in a speech contest. You can change lives when you speak, and you can do it in just 7 minutes.

## Why 7 minutes . . . ?

I have Toastmasters to thank for that! In this book, you'll hear me mention Toastmasters frequently. Toastmasters International is a public speaking organisation which trains members in public speaking and leadership. They have approximately 13,000 clubs and over 270,000 members around the world. Each club has an average of 20 to 30 members.

The first few times I went to Toastmasters, I just sat and watched other club members deliver their speeches. After two weeks, I was ready to join them on stage. I paid my membership fees at Croydon Communicators and David Thompson, a seasoned Toastmaster, handed me the beginners' manual. My goal was to finish the ten tasks from the manual and leave with a certificate – the sooner this happened, the better! Football was my priority; I had yet to fall in love with speaking at the time.

I asked David, "What's next?" and he replied, "All you need to do is give a set of 7 minutes speeches. We are all here to support you." I said, "7 minutes for a speech? That's a bit short!" He replied, "It takes a lot of skill to hold an audience for even a few minutes. 7 minutes will teach you the basics of public speaking – it is the perfect foundation to begin your journey as a speaker."

> "It takes a lot of skill to hold an audience for even a few minutes. 7 minutes will teach you the basics of public speaking – it is the perfect foundation to begin your journey as a speaker."

I was not convinced but then I took the stage and realised two things: first, when you have a lot to say, it takes skill and discipline to stick to a 7 minute time frame. At a Toastmasters club, there is a member sitting at the back of the room who times your speech. The "timer" holds up green, yellow and red cards, which represent the start, half-way and end parts of your 7 minutes. When you see the red card, you must wrap up quickly. This timing system helps you to cut out all the jargon in your speaking and get to the point.

Secondly, I realised that 7 minutes can be a long time when you don't have a lot to say! There have been times when I have arrived at a club meeting without proper preparation, and on the inside I struggled with how I was going to fill 7 minutes. After being in this position time after time, I found that my creative muscles started to flex and I was able to speak spontaneously – somehow it all seemed to make sense once the words came out!

If you go to YouTube and watch any live speeches, the speakers usually switch from story to story, or story to analogy, every 5 to 7 minutes. It would be hard to find a quality speaker that doesn't do this. They are using some of the tools you'll pick up in this book and following what I call the "7 minute formula".

Speaking in a 7 minute time frame taught me to be disciplined and spontaneous. If you are speaking over a longer period of time, try splitting the speech into 7 minute segments and focusing on perfecting each 7 minutes. The more impact, ignition and inspiration you have in your 7 minutes, the easier it is for your audience to stay with you on the journey.

## More on Toastmasters

Toastmasters hosts two main speech contests every year – the Humorous Speech Contest in the autumn and the International Speech Contest in spring. Both competitions start at club level and move up through to area, division and district levels. The Humorous contest finishes at district level, whereas the district winner of the International contest proceeds to the Semi-finals of the World Championship of Public Speaking (usually in the US), and if successful goes on to take the stage at the finals as one of only nine contestants.

Around 25,000 people across the world enter the International Speech contest every year. My contest journey began with the Humorous Speech Contest in September 2010 where I reached the division level, before entering the International Speech Contest the following year.

> "Toastmasters is a great organisation with plenty of opportunity to grow and develop in public speaking and leadership."

Toastmasters is a great organisation with plenty of opportunity to grow and develop in public speaking and leadership. If I hadn't joined Toastmasters at my wife's suggestion, I wouldn't have grown as much in my speaking and this book wouldn't exist! You can find out more about Toastmasters by visiting www.toastmasters.org.

## Your roadmap for *7 Minutes to Win It*

*7 Minutes to Win It* contains tools and techniques that will help you to **impact, ignite** and **inspire** your audience. You will learn how to write and a deliver a speech that will *win* every time – even if you are not in a competition!

The book is written in four parts: Part 1 takes you behind the scenes of my winning speech, Keep on Walking, and the 41 tools and techniques that helped me to make it a winning speech. In Part 2, you will discover my 7 minute formula for success, the power of personal stories and how to grow as a speaker. Part 3 gives you the chance to create your own 7 minute masterpiece, including delivery and evaluation techniques; and finally Part 4 contains transcripts of award-winning speeches from speech champions, as well as useful resources to further your speaking growth.

I've included everything I learned about speaking within a 7 minute time frame in this book – I do not hold back at all. These principles are transferable to keynote speeches, after-dinner speeches, and especially, contest speeches. If you desire to be a speaker that creates and deliver speeches with greater ease and engages your audience intellectually and emotionally each time you speak, *7 Minutes to Win It* is for you.

So if you're ready, let's get started – it's time to win!

# PART 1:
## WINNING BEHIND THE SCENES

There is a definite mindset and process to developing and
delivering a winning speech.

This section will take you behind the scenes into the two dimensions of winning,
how I wrote my own winning speech *Keep on Walking,* and the 41 tools and
techniques that helped me to make it possible.

# CHAPTER 1:

## THE TWO DIMENSIONS OF WINNING

When it comes to public speaking, I believe that winning is everything! You might think that's harsh, brash, and not very British, but allow me to explain. When I was a young footballer, I had that "you must win" mindset, and I won trophies. When I entered the UK and Ireland contest, that voice followed me and it helped me to win the championship – this mindset was the catalyst that helped fuel my passion and with my goal in sight, I practiced more, read more, and gave more on stage.

Winning is different for everyone. For you, winning may be stepping on the stage and overcoming your fear of public speaking. For someone else, it could be sharing a difficult message or even just sharing a 7 minute speech. But if you're going to win in your speaking, it's important that you have a goal, a desire to win (or accomplish that goal) and act on that desire.

For me, when it comes to public speaking, there are two dimensions of winning – winning the honours and winning the hearts.

> "When it comes to public speaking, there are two dimensions of winning – winning the honours and winning the hearts."

### Winning the honours

In 2010, I entered my first speech contest by accident. I was intending to give a speech called *The Laws of the Playground* at my regular Toastmasters meeting. This speech would have been the fourth in the series of ten speeches from the beginners' manual.

That evening, I arrived at the club not knowing that there was anything special about the day. When I asked the Toastmaster if I could make my fourth speech, he said, "Malachi, there will be no formal speeches today. If you want to speak, you must enter the contest." It turned out that this was the day of the Humorous Speech Contest so I agreed to enter because I really just wanted to finish my manual. To my surprise, I ended up winning!

After I spoke, the announcer said, "Malachi will now represent the club at area level." A week later I was the area champion and then I reached the division final! All this was a great experience – I received certificates; I was interviewed by local newspapers and I was celebrated by my club members – I had won the honours!

I won the honours again a few months later in the International Speech Contest, but on a bigger scale. I received several trophies along the way, I was interviewed in more newspapers, on the radio, and even on television, and eventually I was flown to Las Vegas for the World Semi-finals – I was a "H-list" celebrity!

These are the honours of winning a speech contest, and they come with their own benefits: it's incredible for your self-esteem – it feels great to be affirmed and acknowledged by other speakers, and it is wonderful for family and friends to see your hard work pay off. However, winning the honours is not the only way to win.

## Winning the hearts

You can win the hearts of your audience without winning the honours of the contest. The first and second rounds of the International Speech Contest were very different from the Humorous contest. It required that you *inspire* your audience – a concept that was new to me at the time.

With each round, I was growing in confidence, but the third round meant a bigger crowd than I had ever faced before. I'll never forget that day: the contest was held in Marlow in April, 2011. I stepped on the platform and delivered my speech, Keep on Walking. After leaving the stage, I approached David Thompson, a fellow club member, during a break before the results were announced. I asked David if he thought I did well (what I really wanted to know was if he thought I had won!). He said, "Malachi, I have been speaking to people during the break and they told me that your words have inscribed a message on their hearts. They keep saying, 'I am going to keep on walking, just like that young man.'"

I realised at that moment that I had won. Even if the announcer didn't call my name, even if the judges didn't agree, even if I didn't receive a trophy, I had succeeding in winning the hearts of my audience, by inspiring them. Even without a trophy,

> **"Many contestants walk away from a contest feeling upset because they didn't win the honours, not realising that their words may have touched someone's soul."**

I wouldn't be leaving empty handed. Winning the hearts is the second dimension of winning. Many contestants walk away from a contest feeling upset because they didn't win the honours, not realising that their words may have touched someone's soul. For me, I get no better pleasure than an audience member telling me that their life has changed as a result of something I said.

You may be thinking, "Malachi is only saying that because he has won both the honours and the hearts!" But at the Semi-finals in Las Vegas, I came in third place – I didn't reach the final, but again another conversation with a fellow Toastmaster made me feel like a World Champion. I stepped off the platform with my third-place trophy, and a grey-haired lady approached me and said, "Young man, I heard you speak several times in previous rounds and I have heard this speech before, but today you truly touched me. I know what I need to do now. I have a tunnel I have been facing and, today, you helped me." Humbled, I said, "thank you." She replied, "No, thank you."

*That* was my championship moment.

## The quickest way to grow

Entering the speech contest brought out the best in me – the preparation, practice and pressure meant that I would need to dig deep to be successful.

After I won at the district stage, I began to take my practice to a whole new level altogether. I would practice my speech at least 15 times a day, and I started to learn different ways to practice a speech – how to ad-lib when you've lost your words, how to monitor your body language and performance, how to self-evaluate and much more. But I knew there was still another level of speaking, new skills to gain and more effective delivery methods.

I knew I needed to be better. I needed more knowledge, advice, and evaluations, especially if I was going to stand any chance of winning the World Championship.

My district success meant I would be going to Las Vegas to speak on the international stage. I had never spoken internationally before and I would be competing against speakers from all around the world who had also won their own district contests. Because of my winning mindset and desire to improve, I wanted to know how to compete at that level. I sought assistance from Jim Key, the 2003 World Champion of Public Speaking, and Phillip Khan-Panni, World Champion of Public Speaking first runner-up (1995) and three-time Toastmasters UK and Ireland Speech Contest champion.

From Jim and Phillip I learned many valuable speaking techniques, including how to use props effectively, how to gesture, how to use the stage, how to react to laughter, how to pause, and much more. I also bought speech contest videos and books on public speaking – I was a public speaking junkie! I dedicated myself to speaking so much that in those nine months, I can't remember even kicking a football once! I ate, slept and dreamt public speaking and as a result, I grew so much as a speaker.

The contest preparation had me reading things I wouldn't usually read and watching things I wouldn't usually watch, which had a major effect when I took the stage. I could tell from my audiences' reactions and feedback that I had grown as a speaker. The contest (and my winning mindset) forced me to create a culture of learning and practice, and by the end, I was five times the speaker I used to be!

> "The contest preparation had me reading things I wouldn't usually read and watching things I wouldn't usually watch, which had a major effect when I took the stage."

## Win every time

I used to think that public speaking contests were just about the honours but this mindset made me miss the pleasure of moving my audience and prevented me from seeing my growth as a speaker. Thank God I have shifted my thinking!

Believing that winning is only one-dimensional is counterproductive – it creates pressure and limits the growth and impact that you could have as a speaker. You can win not only the honours, but also the hearts of your audience and the added bonus of your own personal growth. Strive to win every time you take the stage and your audience will thank you for it.

# CHAPTER 2:

## DEVELOPING MY WINNING SPEECHES

Until recently, I never wrote down any of my speeches in full on a piece of paper. For some reason, I've always hated the thought of writing speeches out word for word; instead I wrote on scraps of paper that I would eventually lose or drown in the washing machine. This was until I discovered the power of writing out a speech.

I had been in two speech contests at the time and just won the International Speech Contest at the district stage when I asked Jim Key to coach me. Jim said, "That's fine, Malachi, send me a script of your speech." I quickly had to get writing! I had scraps of paper filled with ideas but not a formal script.

As I embarked on this new challenge, I discovered that writing my speech out word for word unlocked my creativity: I noticed words that were redundant and could be cut from the script; I saw opportunities to deepen my connection with my audience, and I learnt how to stay on time. Through this process I discovered that I speak about 110 to 120 words per minute and so I needed to write around 820 words or less to ensure my speech could be delivered in 7 minutes. This is useful to know because it now means I can perform a simple word count on any speech I write to know how much time I will have to deliver it.

> "I discovered that writing my speech out word for word unlocked my creativity . . . I saw opportunities to deepen my connection with my audience . . ."

Writing my speech out also made it evident where to use some of the enhancing techniques I outline in Chapter 4, including where to pause, where and how to utilise vocal variety, and how to use the stage – I can't believe I was missing all these benefits of writing down my speeches!

I now write all my 7 minute speeches down; however, I don't have the same approach when speaking outside the 7 minute time frame, because I would be writing forever!

## Winning speech 1: The Laws of the Playground (2010)

The Laws of the Playground was my entry into the Humorous Speech Contest and my fourth speech as a Toastmaster. I wrote this speech for the fourth assignment in the Toastmasters manual which was entitled, "How to say it". The overall objective was to entertain, using rhetorical devices and vivid words to enhance and emphasise ideas, and to eliminate jargon and word wastage as much as possible.

I had prepared this speech for an ordinary club meeting but when I arrived to deliver it, I discovered it was contest day! I was desperate to speak because I had not spoken at the club in a long time, and I was anxious to complete the ten manual tasks within the one year deadline I had set myself. The organiser told me that if I wanted to speak, I would need to compete in the contest or wait another few weeks to speak again. With no other choice I entered the contest and left the stage the club champion.

The Laws of the Playground was based around one crazy day at the primary school where I work (you can find the transcript in Part 4). In preparation I read children's books to open my imagination and I kept note of funny things that happened at school (children's books are great resources because they have vivid word pictures, good character descriptions, simple language, and very effective structures). I also revisited my childhood memories and almost became a kid again! After about two weeks of reading and making notes, I had crafted a speech on several pieces of paper.

> "Children's books are great resources because they have vivid word pictures, good character descriptions, simple language, and very effective structures."

In the days leading up to the contest, I focused on my delivery. I gathered props, dressed up, took stage in my living room and started to speak. Hours went by and

I enjoyed every second – this was fun! I loved practicing and going over the words, and I could imagine the faces of my audience and sense their emotions as I spoke. I had not practiced like this before and it was a good thing I did because little did I know that I was going to be in a contest when I showed up at my club. That is one secret of a champion – always practice like you are going to be in a contest so your audience gets your best all the time. If a speaker fails on stage, it's usually because they failed to practice sufficiently.

Ultimately the practice paid off for me and I reached the division final. I still wasn't sitting down and writing out a speech as a whole piece at this time, I just wrote snippets everywhere on bits of paper. Now I laugh at my inexperience but back then I didn't see the point of putting pen to paper as I was more inclined to improvise on stage. Things started to change however with my next speech . . .

## Winning speech 2: Keep on Walking (2011)

I wrote a first draft of Keep on Walking in about five days and I had it perfected in two months! I had this draft in a rough version on several pieces of paper all over the house, at school, and in my trouser pockets. My little scraps of paper became a running joke with my friends and family! Little did they (or I for that matter) know that Keep on Walking would become the winning speech of the UK and Ireland International Speech Contest!

My competition speech was the tenth task from the Toastmasters beginners' manual which meant that after delivering this, I would officially be known as a "Competent Communicator". If I decided to progress further, I could work my way through the advanced manuals.

I used the suggested number 10 speech structure, which simply instructs to speak with passion to inspire and unify the audience. I knew that, unlike the humorous contest, I would need to speak from a place deep within me. Not that I wouldn't need to add a little humour, but I would need to share my life – not just a joke or two.

In my time of preparation, I did a lot of reflection and questioning – I was waiting for a message to come. I tried to remember the worst things that have happened to me and the life episodes that taught me the biggest lessons. I remembered a racist attack I had suffered when I was a young boy. I also recalled what it was like growing up without a father in the early stages of my life and I thought of what life was like when my dad returned. Finally I thought of the one big lesson I learned throughout these experiences, a gift I could offer my audience as the take home message.

After writing down my ideas, I gave an early form of the speech to my Year 6 group at school (10-11 year olds). The silence after was

> "After writing down my ideas, I gave an early form of Keep on Walking to my Year 6 group at school. The silence after was deafening — I knew then that I had something powerful."

deafening — I knew then that I had something powerful. The students asked me questions and gave me feedback, which helped me to understand the emotion that my speech carried. I won the contest at club level and from this point, it took about two months to perfect the speech. Keep on Walking grew each time I gave it — this was a speech that started out on scraps of paper but is now written on people's hearts.

## Moving up the ranks

There are great speakers at every level of the International Speech Contest but the quality of speaking generally tends to improve with each level. As they ascend through the ranks, the contestants improve all aspects of their speaking including delivery, structure, and humour. By the time I got to the semi-finals, every single speech I heard was exceptional.

One of the main reasons speeches improve incrementally is that preparation time between each level increases as contestants move up the ranks. This ranges from two weeks between club and area levels and two to three months between the district and semi-finals.

## A word of advice: don't compare, prepare!

If you're thinking of entering a speech contest, here's a word of advice — don't compare, prepare! I was anticipating that there would be great speakers at the semi-final level so I watched some online videos of some of the contestants. This can be very intimidating, especially when you are a young man with a tendency to compare yourself!

I fell into the comparison trap — I started looking at other speakers and questioning whether I was better than one person or worse than the next. Of course, that kind of thinking got me nowhere fast. It made my speech more about the contest than the crowd, more about me than my audience. I became frustrated and during that period I stopped enjoying my speaking.

And then one day my earlier experience came back to me. I remembered that whether or not I won, I had touched people's hearts in the past and the semi-final contest was just another opportunity to touch more hearts on a larger scale. My priorities properly realigned and I decided to just go out there and give my speech, and my audience, my best. I started intense preparation, forgetting about the other speakers and focusing instead on my audience and my message. When I made the shift from comparing to preparing, I started to enjoy the journey once more.

> **"When I made the shift from comparing to preparing, I started to enjoy the journey once more."**

Comparison is destructive. Always remember that you have a gift, a talent and a message — your job is simply to take your best to the stage every time you speak.

# Keep on Walking

### Winning speech by Malachi Talabi

### 2011 District 71 (UK & Ireland) International Speech Champion

When life throws its worst at you, you only have two choices: to stay trapped in a tunnel or to keep on walking.

Mr. Contest Chair, ladies and gentlemen, and anyone who's ever been hit where it hurts, life threw its worst at me when I stood face to face with Terry in the tunnel.

It wasn't strange for me to walk home on my own from school; my dad was in Nigeria and had been for 10 years, and my mum was a black statistic – a benefit beggar, single parent, three children, working hard to put cream crackers on the table or pay the electricity. It was never both.

I came out of Bermondsey station, walked pass the bus stop, and peered into the tunnel. I saw Terry and his mate inside. Terry was freckled-faced and filled with fury. He had bruised, battered knuckles. He was 18 years old and he *hated* ten year olds, especially black Africans.

My heart started to beat as I entered the tunnel. The next thing I remember is Terry grabbing me.

*Terry*: "I hate you, I hate you!" *(\*spits\*)*

*Terry's friend*: "Terry, someone's coming, let's go!"

I laid there in a pool of blood. Terry had made a mess of my face; I felt like my face was in a frying pan.

Has life ever thrown a punch at *you* that you weren't prepared for?

I got up, wiped away the blood and his spit, and I kept on walking.

A few years later, I was in secondary school. The first day was good, the second day was OKAY, but by the third day . . . the bullying began.

I went to Saint Thomas the Apostle school — we called it "bully central". Mum was putting cream crackers on the table or paying the electricity — it was never both! No electricity meant no washing machine, and no washing machine meant that I stank!

And on the third day, it was time for P.E. and I had to take my blazer off.

*School classmates*: "Arrrgh you stink! Talabi you reek! You smell worse than rat's vomit! In fact, you smell soooo bad, you make Right Guard want to go left!"

It was just like being back in the tunnel again with Terry.

"You stink, you smell, I hate you!"

I couldn't deny it — you could see the dirt around my collar and the damp circles underneath my arm pits. I was no longer the black boy from Bermondsey, I was now the black boy from Bermondsey with B.O.

It's OKAY, I can laugh about it now too . . . has anyone ever said anything to *you* that shattered your self-esteem?

I got up, wiped away the shame, and I kept on walking.

College was amazing! The sun shone and I smiled; the bus came and I caught it; Mum was putting cream crackers on the table *and* paying the electricity — it was both!

Everything was okay . . . until results day.

I walked up to the deadly desk to discover *(bring folded paper out of pocket)* my results were miles away from an A — what was I going to tell my mum?

"Err Mum, here are my results."

*Mum*: "Oh my God! I cooked for you, I cleaned for you . . . go and tell your dad!"

"Dad's back?" I hadn't seen him in 18 years. I wondered what he looked like.

"Dad, here are my results . . ."

*Dad:* "My son, you are silly, you are stupid and you are slothful; get out of my sight!"

I was back in the tunnel again.

Has a family member ever turned their back on *you*?

Ladies and gentlemen, this time when I was in the tunnel, I didn't see a wimp, I saw a winner. You see, I could have stayed there with my jaw against the floor, with shame in my veins, the smell of blood in my nostrils, and fear doing a disco in my mind.

But I refused to stay down, I refused to stay defeated, I refused to remain in pain.

You see, I didn't let racism ruin me, I kept on walking; I didn't let bullying beat me, I kept on walking; I didn't let neglect knock me out, I kept on walking.

Walking through my tunnels, I have become an author; walking through my tunnels, I have become a football coach; walking through my tunnels, I have become a speaker because now I have things to say.

There is nothing you can't become or overcome if you keep on walking.

You see our tunnels make us, our tunnels mould us, our tunnels help us realise our potential for greatness.

Maybe you're here today because you're trapped in a tunnel; maybe you've lost your confidence; maybe you've lost your job or a loved one and it's dark and it's cold, and you're hurting. I encourage you to keep on walking, because I have discovered that every cloud has a silver lining and there is light at the end of every tunnel.

When life throws its worst at you, you only have two choices. What will *you* decide? To stay trapped in a tunnel or to keep on walking?

# CHAPTER 3:

## KEEP ON WALKING – MINUTE BY MINUTE

In a speech contest, you only have 7 minutes to win the honours and the hearts of your audience. Every second counts, which means that every word counts! Every word, action and gesture must be planned because they can either work for you or against you. In the next chapter I will take you behind the scenes of Keep on Walking and show you the thinking, techniques and tools behind the speech; but first, we'll analyse the speech minute-by-minute in this chapter.

### Making a long story short

I have spoken to many speakers who say, "Malachi, my story is so long, how can I keep it to just 7 minutes?" My response is simple: always think about what can be cut – not everything in your story is important to your message, and not every detail in your story needs to be told. If you want to tell a story and leave a strong message, always ask yourself, "What can I cut?"

> **"If you want to tell a story and leave a strong message, always ask yourself, 'What can I cut?'"**

In Keep on Walking, many things happened to me between my primary school and university but I didn't include them all because they didn't support my message. I had three short stories in the speech but none of them were more than two minutes long – it is important to be able to tell a short story effectively and concisely, especially in the 7 minute time frame.

To be efficient in your word count and storytelling, you must first ask, "What can I cut?" Then you should ask, "What must I add?" (for example, important dates and facts surrounding your story.) In my first story, I use alliteration, word pictures and dialogue to move along faster and give the audience a clear sense of the scene without too many words and details. Most people have two minutes to spare – practice telling your short story to friends, family, even work colleagues, and keep on telling it until you've whittled it down to its most significant points. Then begin to add the relevant techniques to enhance your delivery. Remember, you've got about two and a half minutes to play with for one short story.

### Minute 1: Establishing the setting

I start my speech with a pause and then engage the audience with a challenging statement, *"When life throws its worst at you . . ."* I set the scene and introduce the main characters and the circumstances of my life, including the conflict of being poor and facing a bully. I stand planted in the middle of the stage for this setting.

### Minute 2: The first question

This is an action scene – I face my bully and I am beaten up. I use dialogue to describe the encounter with my bully; I use my bag as a prop and then I ask the audience my first question: *"Has life ever thrown a punch at you that you weren't prepared for?"* When I ask this question, I am planted in the middle of the stage.

### Minute 3: Transition to another story

I transition to my second story by picking up my school bag as a prop. I change both the emotions and the timeline by saying, *"College is amazing . . ."* This story too is full of dialogue.

### Minute 4: The half-way point humour

At the halfway point, I am telling the second story using dialogue. As I've built tension in the emotional journey through the first half, this is where I use the first piece of humour to lighten the mood. The audience sniggers at the statement, "I was no longer the black boy from Bermondsey, I was now the black boy from Bermondsey with B.O." I end the story with a question and my foundational phrase.

### Minute 5: The climactic scene

In the fifth minute, I tell the third short story. I change emotions in the speech by describing how much fun I had at college and I show this with my facial expressions (I smile). I then introduce my twist — my results are not good. I use accents and a lot of dialogue in this scene. This is the climactic scene of my speech. When I'm showing my results to my mum and dad, I ask two questions to engage the audience: 1) *"What was I going to tell my mum?"* 2) *"Dad's back? I hadn't seen him in 18 years."*

### Minute 6: The conclusion

This is the beginning of the end; I don't use any more dialogue from here until the end. I raise the tone of my voice and describe how I overcame my obstacles. I use my foundational phrase frequently at this point and I begin to use call backs to reference the previous minutes. I move around the stage and make eye contact with audience members to share my passion.

### Minute 7: Call to action

At the very end of the speech, I lower the tone of my voice and call my audience to action with a question. I am planted back in the middle of the stage at this point.

## Summary

Now that you've seen the minute by minute breakdown, let's sum it up: it's important to learn how to tell short stories; it's equally important to have quick seamless transitions because a bumpy transition can ruin your speech. The climactic scene is a powerful place in your speech because this is the scene that your audience have been waiting for. When you deliver this scene, commit to every gesture and every movement and remember to pause where necessary. If you've taken your audience on an emotional journey that involves heart and humour, by the time you reach your conclusion your audience will be ready for your call to action and by the time you deliver your call to action, they will be ready to make a decision.

In the next chapter you will pick up 41 tools and techniques that will help you get the edge in your speaking. But even as you learn and apply them, remember: emotional connection wins over techniques so always aim for the hearts of your audience.

# CHAPTER 4:

## BEHIND THE SCENES – TOOLS AND TECHNIQUES OF A MAGIC SCRIPT

Every quality speech has particular similarities. In this chapter I have narrowed down all the tools and techniques I used in Keep on Walking, which I have also observed in other winning speeches.

Each tool or technique is explained in glossary format and then followed by a demonstration of how I used it in Keep on Walking. They are in no particular order of importance, rather I tried to approach it as logically as possible from the beginning of my script to the end. Use as many as possible to help you in your next speech. If applied correctly, these tools and techniques can enhance your delivery, clarify your message, and engage your audience.

## Coaching

It's important to mention this first because I believe coaching is incredibly valuable. Jim Key and Phillip Khan-Panni helped me with Keep on Walking. I spent a lot of time working with Jim over the internet and face-to-face in Las Vegas, soaking up his priceless advice like a sponge. Jim was a fantastic coach – he focused more on my growth as a speaker than my success in the competition. He taught me that humour is important to help balance the emotions in a speech.

Phillip was also excellent – he taught me the secrets of using vocal variety and props in unique ways. He also shared with me writing and memorisation techniques that I still use today. Without a coach, I would still have given a passionate message, but I can sincerely say that these coaches helped me turn my passion into a powerful presentation.

> "I recommend coaching if you want to speak professionally or compete in a contest. In fact, if you want to take your speaking to the next level, coaching is your elevator."

I recommend coaching if you want to speak professionally or compete in a contest. In fact, if you want to take your speaking to the next level, coaching is your elevator.

## Your speech title

Your speech title can tease, tickle, twist, or act as a trailer for your speech (see Chapter 9 for more on this). You can also use your speech title as a *foundational phrase*, a catchphrase, or a "golden thread", which repeats throughout your speech. A familiar example of a golden thread is from the story of The Three Little Pigs where the wolf repeatedly says, "I'll huff and I'll puff and I'll blow your house down."

Your speech title is important and how you use it can depend on the type of speech you are writing. For example, if your speech is humorous, then it helps to have a funny title to help your audience anticipate your humour; if your speech is inspirational, you may want your title be a clever metaphor of your message. Your title could also be the name of a place or a date that sets the stage for your speech – whatever it is, use your title as a tool to your advantage.

### My speech title: Keep on Walking

I chose Keep on Walking because I liked that it was short, simple and easy to remember. It also supports the metaphor of movement and the physical gestures of walking that I use in my delivery. My title was one of the most powerful tools I used to help my message stick with my audience – in fact, during my speech, I repeated the phrase Keep on Walking nine times!

It became what 1999 World Champion of Public Speaking, Craig Valentine, calls a "foundational phrase" – a phrase upon which the message is encapsulated. The impact of a good speech title will be obvious when an audience member remembers it months after hearing you speak, which I've experienced many times with Keep on Walking. I made my speech hard to forget by using my title as a foundational phrase.

# Introduction

Your introduction is important because it's your first chance to make an impression on your audience. In a Toastmasters speech contest, contestants are usually expected to greet the Toastmaster and the audience. Although this is an expectation and not a rule, I believe it is a good idea to greet those to whom you are speaking, as long as it's not done in a clichéd way.

> **"Your introduction is important because it's your first chance to make an impression on your audience."**

When you first greet the audience, saying predicable things like, "Thank you for having me", or "Hello, my name is Bob", can make for a very boring start. As soon as an audience hears a cliché, they mentally switch off so when giving your greetings, tuck them in within a story, statement or a question. Read Chapter 5 to learn how to start your speech with S.P.I.C.E.

### My introduction

*"Mr. Contest Chair, ladies and gentlemen, and anyone who's ever been hit where it hurts, life threw its worst at me when I stood face to face with Terry in the tunnel."*

In my introduction, I make a statement and then issue my formal greeting which sounds conversational. In fact, in Windsor, the Toastmasters International President, Pat Johnson, was present in the audience so I changed the introduction to say, "Madame President, ladies and gentlemen . . ."

Jim Key suggested using the rule of three to cover all bases of the audience, instead of the potentially lengthy equivalent of acknowledging everyone present by name or title ((see below for more on the rule of three). With this rule of three introduction, I covered all sections of the audience easily and succinctly, and the last sentence of my introduction – ". . . anyone who has ever been hit where it hurts . . ." – helps with the transition into the first story of the body.

## Story structure

Every story needs a structure, and the most common structure is beginning, middle and end. Most audiences will easily follow this structure, however you don't always need to be this linear – you can start at the end of your story and work backwards to the beginning. Another option is to use the 'problem-cause-solution' structure where you start with a problem, mention the cause and in your conclusion offer a solution. Different structures can add a unique dimension to your storytelling.

> "Different story structures can add a unique dimension to your storytelling."

### My story structure

My story was structured traditionally in the beginning, middle and end format. I establish the setting by introducing the main characters and sharing my life experiences.

## The message

The message is the underlying point or lesson of your speech. The message is sometimes relayed in a sentence near the beginning or end of the speech when the speaker sums up his or her story.

### My message

*"I encourage you to keep on walking, because I have discovered that every cloud has a silver lining, and there is light at the end of every tunnel."*

In these lines I am passionate in my delivery because I know the power of words, but I am also very sensitive in my vocal tone when I deliver these lines. I add the words "encourage you" before "keep on walking" because I understand that walking is hard when you are bruised by life. This is my message summed up with the lesson I have learned. I repeat my speech title and foundational phrase, and I use the familiar image of a light at the end of the tunnel to create a word picture.

## Foundational phrase (catchphrase)

The term foundational phrase is coined by Craig Valentine, although many speakers use it and refer to it as a catchphrase. A foundational phrase is a short phrase that sums up your entire message. These phrases help your audience to remember your speech long after you've spoken, just like Dr. Martin Luther King Jr.'s foundational phrase, "I have a dream". Repetition is important to establish your foundational phrase.

### My foundational phrase

*"When life throws its worst at you, you only have two choices. What will you decide? To stay trapped in a tunnel or to **keep on walking**?"*

I used my speech title as a foundational phrase and I repeat this several times throughout the speech, including the end. This helps to embed my message in the minds of my audience members.

## Chronological order

You may choose to tell your story in chronological order based on time – from the earliest date to the latest.

### My chronological order

*"It wasn't strange for me to walk home on my own from school . . ."*

*"A few years later I was in secondary school . . ."*

*"College was amazing!"*

I told my story in chronological order with transitions to lead the audience through my story. Notice that I went from primary school, to secondary school, then college.

## Emotional journey

Emotions of happiness, sadness, fear, joy, pain, loss, and sorrow are all common feelings which can form part of the emotional journey. The emotions and the sequence of the emotions you evoke within your speech represent the emotional journey on which you are taking your audience. It's important to be aware of what emotions you transmit during your speech.

> "The emotions and the sequence of the emotions you evoke within your speech represent the emotional journey on which you are taking your audience."

### My emotional journey

*"The sun shone and I smiled* (big smile) *..."*

By this point, I have taken my audience down emotionally. The speech has been very intense so far; now is the time to release the tension so I deliver this line in a very upbeat and positive manner.

*'Mum (in dramatic African accent): "Oh my God! I cooked for you, I cleaned for you ... go and tell your dad!"*

This is the climactic scene of my speech. I decided to utilise dialogue (see below) to really bring out my characters and enhance the intensity of the emotional journey. I am using dialogue which keeps the speech short and conveys more emotion than you would achieve by just retelling the story with no dialogue. My audience is able to feel the pain of my mother and my own personal disappointment.

## Empathy

As a speaker you can let your audience know that you empathise with them through your body language (eye contact) and tone of voice. This helps build a strong connection.

### My empathy

*". . . maybe you've lost your job or a loved one and **it's dark and it's cold, and you're hurting**."*

I deliver this line with a soft tone of voice; I describe a tunnel to show that I know just how they might feel as I was once in that tunnel myself.

## Scenarios

Speakers can use scenarios to connect with an audience. Scenarios can help build the emotional journey and create identification with the speaker. If an audience member is going through or has gone through a scenario you create, they will be able to easily relate to you and understand your message.

### My scenarios

*"**Maybe you're** here today because you're trapped in a tunnel; **maybe you've** lost your confidence; **maybe you've** lost your job or a loved one and it's dark and it's cold, and you're hurting . . ."*

I paint three different real life scenarios here while repeating my tunnel metaphor and utilising the power of three. These are scenarios that my audience may be facing or have already faced. I use the word "maybe" here to not be overly forceful with my message and not to presume about my audience's lives — too many speakers presume too much!

## Pause power

The pause is powerful. Pausing deepens your connection with your audience and makes you come across as more sincere. When you pause your audience thinks, reflects, digests, laughs, and anticipates what will happen next.

> "Pausing deepens your connection with your audience and makes you come across as more sincere."

The pause, if used correctly, is an extremely powerful tool for a speaker. If your audience is laughing or clapping, you should be pausing. Strategically planning other pauses throughout your speech is also important.

### My pause power

Before starting Keep on Walking, I paused, smiled, and made eye contact with my audience members — this is a great way to start your speech.

*"Terry was freckled-faced and filled with fury. He had bruised, battered knuckles. He was 18 years old and he hated ten year olds, especially* (pause) *black Africans.* (pause)*"*

I pause for effect before saying "especially black Africans", and I pause after saying it. When I pause the second time, I point to myself to indicate I was the subject. I paused here because I had given a lot of information, some of it negative, and I wanted my audience to digest these words and feel the emotions behind them. Again, when I paused, I made eye contact with a member of the audience deliberately to deepen the impact and connection of my words.

*"Everything was OKAY . . . until results day* (pause)*"*

By adding a pause, this line adds suspense and curiosity leading up to the next big twist. After releasing the tension in the next few lines, I move back to building up to a climactic finish. This is a good example of how the pause can enhance your story and its drama.

## The power of "you"

I believe that "you" is the most powerful word in public speaking. Apart from using the names of audience members in your speech "you" is the greatest way to make your speech personal. "You" is more personal than "we" or "us"; it is conversational and gives your audience the impression that you are speaking to them individually. If you write your speech with "you" in mind, you will be far ahead of most other speakers who use "we", "us" and "I".

> **"Apart from using the names of audience members in your speech, 'you' is the greatest way to make your speech personal."**

### My power of you

*"When life throws its worst at you, you only have two choices: to stay trapped in a tunnel or to keep on walking."*

I decided to use "you" here to shift the focus from me and grab my audience's attention immediately. I changed the opening line from the original, "If anybody has ever been stuck in a tunnel . . ." to "When life throws its worst at *you* . . ." to make my opening more impactful.

*". . . you could see the dirt around my collar* (hold the collar) *and the damp circles underneath my arm pits* (raise arms)."

I use "you" here to draw my audience into my story. I then start to paint pictures in their minds – an audience member may, at this point, be thinking about how dirty they too looked during their own school days. In earlier drafts of the speech, instead of "damp circles", I said ". . . yellow circles underneath my armpits," but one evaluator said that this description was too graphic and almost repulsive, so I replaced that line. This illustrates the importance of evaluation which we will discuss later.

*"There is nothing you can't become or overcome if you keep on walking."*

In my conclusion, I relate the whole speech back to the audience using the word "you", ensuring that the speech is not just about me and what I went through but also about my audience and empathising with whatever their situation may be.

## You-focused questions

Craig Valentine also coined the term, "you-focused question", referring to questions that address the audience directly. These are questions such as, "Have you ever felt life is not fair?" or, "What would you do if you were locked out of your house and the landlord is on holiday?"

> "You-focused questions shift your audience's attention and reflection away from you and onto themselves . . ."

You-focused questions help make your speech more conversational and allow your audience to better reflect on your message. These types of questions shift the audience's attention and reflection away from you and onto themselves – this gives the impression that your speech is a tool to help the audience rather than a therapy session for you as a speaker!

### My you-focused questions

*"Has life ever thrown a punch at **you** that **you** weren't prepared for?"*

I have noticed in my speeches that I usually tell three short stories and then end with a question that includes the word "you". I expect my audience to reflect on their own life experiences at this point and when I say this, I again make and hold eye contact with one audience member. It is important to pause and allow the audience to answer the question in their own minds.

Throughout the speech, I strategically ask you-focused questions to help my audience reflect on their life and their circumstances.

## Power question

A power question differs from a normal question or a "you"-focused question. A power question occurs when a speaker asks a question that seems to anticipate what the audience is already thinking. Power questions help you to instantly engage and connect with your audience as they will feel that you are all on the same wavelength.

### My power question

*"I walked up to the deadly desk to discover my results were miles away from an A – **what was I going to tell my mum?**"*

This power question is powerful regardless of whether the audience identify with me or my mum. If they identify with my mum, they may be thinking, "Yeah, I'd like to hear his excuse, too!" If they identify with me, maybe because they have had bad school grades too, they may be thinking, "How is he going to get out of this?"

To increase the effectiveness of this power question, I add the gesture of slightly raising my shoulders and then literally asking what I know they will be thinking: "What *is* he going to tell his mum?"

## Answered questions

Every story will present questions in the minds of audience members. Why did your character make that decision? What motivated that response? How did things end up? Answering questions like who, what, when, where, and why will give your audience a clearer picture of the details of your story.

When you receive an evaluation, take note of any unanswered questions your evaluator raises and make a point to address these in your next draft. Popular questions that need answering include the age of your characters, dates, times and setting.

> **"When you receive an evaluation, take note of any unanswered questions your evaluator raises and make a point to address these in your next draft."**

### My answered questions

"**Terry's mate**: *'Terry, someone's coming, let's go!'*"

I knew my audience would be wondering how my attack at the hands of Terry the bully ended. I needed to answer this question and I did so in this line of dialogue. Further character description of Terry's mate is not important here as he's just a tool to answer the question.

## Specific details

Being specific in providing specific dates, names, places and ages in your speech gives you credibility. However you need to decide which details are the most important to provide, otherwise the specifics might take away from the speech.

### My specifics

*"I went to Saint Thomas the Apostle school — we called it 'bully central.'"*

When you mention specific details in a personal story, it builds the credibility of your message. When I stepped off the platform after giving this speech at the division final, an audience member came up to me and told me that he had been to the same school in a younger age group! We discussed classes we had both taken, which teachers were still present – as a result of my specific details I made a new friend!

## Conflict, curiosity and suspense

Without at least one of these three elements in your speech, you will only be hoping that your audience stays with you as you speak. Why do people watch soap operas, murder mysteries and so on? Simple – because of the conflict, curiosity and suspense! People want to know what happens next and they will hang around to find out what happens. The same principles apply to the stories you tell in your speech.

### My conflict, curiosity and suspense

*"Mr. Contest Chair, ladies and gentlemen, and anyone who's ever been hit where it hurts, life threw its worst at me when I stood face to face with Terry in the tunnel."*

The first two lines of my introduction are full of conflict, curiousity and suspense. These lines make the audience think, "What happened in the tunnel?" "Who is Terry?" – they are already hooked into my story!

## Characters

Every story needs characters – characters help bring your speech to life because audience members will usually relate to particular characters. Characters can also help create humour in your speech. Use characters carefully, however – too many may confuse your story and muddle your message.

> **"Every story needs characters – characters help bring your speech to life . . ."**

### My characters

My mum was one of my main characters. I do not describe her height or hair colour because this is not really important, especially in 7 minutes. Instead, I describe the struggles she faces as this supports the speech and my message. Any mothers in the audience may identify with this character, especially if they have had similar experiences caring for their families.

Terry was another main character in my speech. I remembered what he looked like – I could never forget! I used word pictures to describe him and tied in alliteration to bring the description alive. When I describe Terry as an 18 year old, I raise my hand to indicate that he is older, taller and bigger than me. This helps my audience see the reality of what I faced. Characterisation using gestures, dialogue and accents can bring your characters and speech to life.

## Dialogue

Speakers can give their characters voices through dialogue. Speakers can even use dialogue to share their own thoughts. For example you might say, "I thought, 'I must win this time.'" I have learned not to overdo voice imitations though as they can come across as too showy and may even be distracting to your audience.

### My dialogue

'School classmates (voice change): 'Arrrgh you stink! Talabi you reek! You smell worse than rats vomit! In fact, you smell soooo bad, you make Right Guard want to go left!'"

I love using dialogue because it brings a speech to life! I chose to put the bullying into dialogue but I didn't use a child's voice as this would have been distracting and too much like acting.

## The rule of three

In public speaking, the rule of three describes a trinity of points or words that are easy for an audience to follow and remember. Often, the third point is used as a punch line that the audience will find humorous.

> "In public speaking, the rule of three describes a trinity of points or words that are easy for an audience to follow and remember."

The rule of three has been used and proven throughout history, such as "Friends, Romans, countrymen . . ." in Shakespeare's Julius Caesar play. Also fairytales like The Three Little Pigs, Three Blind Mice, Goldilocks and the Three Bears, and Ebenezer Scrooge's three ghosts of Christmas past, all utilise the rule of three.

People tend to remember things in threes therefore the rule of three is a very effective tool in public speaking.

### My rule of three

*"The first day was good, the second day was okay, but by the third day . . . the bullying began."*

The rule of three is littered throughout my speech; this statement is just one example. This series of three lead the audience through a timeline they can easily understand. I also utilise the power of pause (after the third day in the series) and alliteration to enhance this whole line.

# Humour

Humour is any part of your speech or delivery that makes your audience laugh.

### My humour

*"In fact, you smell soooo bad, you make Right Guard want to go left!"*

Jim Key helped me with this line. Jim taught me that a good inspirational speech needs a balance of humour and seriousness. I included the Right Guard brand because I was sensitive to speaking internationally (more on this later). Right Guard is an American brand of deodorant so this resonated particularly well in the United States at the semi-finals. When using humour it is important that your audience understand your reference. I might change this line at times depending on my audience.

*"(Very softly)* **It's okay, I can laugh about it now too** *. . . has anyone ever said anything to you that shattered your self-esteem?"*

Jim also taught me that sometimes you have to give your audience permission to laugh. He said that it is important to acknowledge the laughter, especially when people are laughing at something that is also serious and painful. Give permission by making a statement, like the one above, and deliver it with a slight smile as the audience may not know it is okay to laugh, or they may feel guilty that they laughed at such an emotional moment.

## Twist

A twist is an unexpected occurrence in a speech, whether as part of a story or your overall message. Twists can be powerful tools because they can bring out humour, shock, surprise or powerful lessons that your audience were not expecting.

> "Twists can be powerful tools because they can bring out humour, shock, surprise or powerful lessons that your audience were not expecting."

### My twist

"Mum (in dramatic African accent): 'Oh my God! I cooked for you, I cleaned for you . . . go and tell your dad!'"

"(looking puzzled) 'Dad's back?' I hadn't seen him in 18 years. I wondered what he looked like."

I grew up without the consistent presence of my father – he was here one minute, gone the next. In my story, I now have to explain my results to him. This line is a twist in the tale which creates conflict and suspense.

## Transition

Transitions act as passageways from one part of a speech to another. Words and phrases such as "a few months later", or "fast forward a few years" can be categorised as transitional phrases. You can fit years into 7 minutes if you have good transitions.

### My transition

"*College was amazing! The sun shone and I smiled* (big smile)"

In 7 minutes I transition from primary school to secondary school and finally to college. Although the anecdotes are years apart, the audience can easily follow the passing of time through the transitional phrase.

# Metaphor

In her book Metaphorically Selling, Anne Miller describes a metaphor as a mental equation in which something is compared to something else. In my speech, the main metaphor was comparing my trauma to a tunnel.

### My metaphor

*"It was **just like** being back in the tunnel again with Terry."*

The tunnel is the metaphor here. Jim Key helped me transform this line – I originally said "I was back in the tunnel again"; however, to support the use of the metaphor, I added the phrase "just like". If I had left it the way it was, I risked my audience mistaking my metaphor.

# Alliteration

Alliteration is defined as the repetition of a particular sound in the first syllables of a series of words or phrases – for example, cool, clever, and concise. When used well, alliteration is like music to an audience's ears, but as with many techniques, too much alliteration can have the opposite effect of being irritating.

> **"When used well, alliteration is like music to an audience's ears, but as with many techniques, too much alliteration can have the opposite effect of being irritating."**

### My alliteration

*". . . my mum was a **black** statistic – a **benefit beggar**, single parent, three children, working hard to put cream crackers on the table or pay the electricity . . ."*

I used a lot of alliteration in Keep on Walking – I find it helps me keep my word count low by efficiently summarising a description in just two or three words, instead of using lengthy sentences.

*"I was no longer the black boy from Bermondsey; I was now the black boy from Bermondsey with B.O."*

I use alliteration here to really drive home the image of how I felt while being bullied. Audiences find this line funny, especially when I was in the United States. It releases the tension of the whole situation and at the midway point in the speech, this is a great place for humour.

*"I walked up to the **deadly desk to discover** my results were miles away from an A . . ."*

I used alliteration here to earn points. In a contest, alliteration works wonders because judges award points based on your use of words.

## Opposites

A speaker can use opposite concepts for dramatic effect such as, "It was the beginning of the end — my enthusiasm went up but my bank balance went down. I felt like a winner but all I could do was lose." Opposites are memorable and help you to summarise your point without over-explaining.

### My opposites

*". . . this time when I was in the tunnel I didn't see a wimp, I saw a winner."*

I use the powers of opposites, word pictures and alliteration here. This helps me to keep my words short and also shows my creativity with words (which helped in the judging criteria).

## Word pictures

Word pictures transport an audience into a scene. They paint a picture in the minds of your audience and helps them to see what you see. For instance, if I were to say to you, "She barked at me like a drunken dog?", what kind of image does that generate in your mind? This is a very strong word picture.

> **"Use word pictures well, but remember you are a speaker, not a poet!"**

Use word pictures well, but remember you are a speaker, not a poet! Experience, evaluations and coaching will help you learn what things you need to describe and what things you don't.

### My word pictures

*"I laid there in a pool of blood. Terry had made a mess of my face . . ."*

Instead of saying I was really hurt, being quite graphic here helps my audience see the scene. I use word pictures frequently to draw my audience in.

## Kinaesthetic statements

A kinaesthetic statement is a phrase used to communicate a feeling which embodies the atmosphere and emotions of you, your character, or a scene. You can use kinaesthetic statements to describe your feelings, draw your audience into the story, and touch their emotions.

Craig Valentine has a speaking formula called 'VAKS' which is an acronym for Visual Auditory Kinaesthetic and Sight. As all audience members have their own unique way of listening and learning, Craig encourages speakers to consider the VAKS in order to touch all five senses during a speech.

Although I wrote Keep on Walking before reading any of Craig's materials, this is still a powerful thing to consider when making your speech more sensory and in hindsight I could see where I had done this unconsciously.

### My kinaesthetic statements

*"I felt like my face was in a frying pan."*

This statement encapsulates my pain into a feeling, allowing the audience to sense how painful Terry's blows were to my 10-year-old body. The added effect of a pause helps this emotion to sink in for the audience.

## Power line

A power line is the combination of a variety of techniques in one line, and as such can be filled with rhythm, rhyme, metaphor and the rule of three. Said with pace and passion it is a treat for your audience.

### My power line

*"But I refused to stay down, I refused to stay defeated, I refused to remain in pain."*

This is one of my favourite lines in the speech, and I delivered it from the heart. As I was writing my speech, it just came out with an ideal mix of the rule of three, repetition, alliteration and rhyme. When I deliver this line, it is packed with passion. I change my tone slightly to emote my pain and determination and because this is near my conclusion, I really go for it! Not shouting, but speaking faster with passion in my voice, followed by a pause.

*"You see, I didn't let racism ruin me, I kept on walking; I didn't let bullying beat me, I kept on walking; I didn't let neglect knock me out, I kept on walking."*

In this line I used call backs to help sum up my speech in a power line. If someone arrived in the middle of my speech they could still understand the essence of my message. I used the rule of three twice here, as well as repetition and rhyme. This one line accomplished so much, and that's why it's a power line. Always enhance your power lines with passion and pace.

*"You see **our tunnels** make us, **our tunnels** mould us, **our tunnels** help us realise our potential for greatness."*

Here I am describing the power of a tunnel, which I can see clearly because I am out of my own tunnel of trauma. This power line delivers the rule of three, metaphors, and word pictures to convey my message. It explains the power of being in a tunnel and getting through it.

## Staging

Staging is simply how you use the physical space of the stage. The techniques used in staging support your delivery and enhance your words. Staging techniques include

**"Staging is simply how you use the physical space of the stage. The techniques used in staging support your delivery and enhance your words."**

where, how, and when to move around the stage. There is more detailed information on various forms of staging in Chapter 10.

### My staging

"(Speaks to mum hesitantly, scratching head) *'Err Mum, here are my results.'*"

I look to the side of the stage when I ask my mum this question, as if she is standing next to me. That part of the stage now represents my mother. I used the stage to plant my character. Although my mother was not visible, my audience knew exactly where she was on the stage.

## Props

Props are any physical object you use to support your speech. As with many techniques discussed here, balance is important – too many props can make a speech look like a stage show and can make you look like an actor instead of a public speaker.

> **Too many props can make a speech look like a stage show and can make you look like an actor instead of a public speaker.**

Props can be a very powerful method of engaging your audience and illustrating your message but be careful which objects you choose as props and how many.

### My props

"(pick up **bag**)"

To deliver Keep on Walking, I dress in a school uniform and have several props on stage. The first prop I use is a school bag which acts as a visual transition to the first stage of my childhood.

*"I walked up to the deadly desk to discover* (bring **folded paper** out of pocket) *my results were miles away from an A . . ."*

I used a white piece of paper to demonstrate my results sheet. This prop continues to work a few lines later, when my dad crumples and throws the paper – the silence is deafening!

## Vocal variety

Using your voice to change the pace of your speech, make a sound effect, or adopt a character keeps an audience's attention and can help them follow along without getting bored. Monotone is a no-no for championship speaking, as is speaking too fast. Strategically plan your pauses, pace, tone, volume and other facets of using your voice to enhance your words.

### My vocal variety

"(quicker) *My heart started to beat as I entered the tunnel* (beat hand on chest). *The next thing I remember is Terry grabbing me.*"

At this point, I increase the pace of my words and beat my hand against my chest. I literally recreate how I felt at the scene.

"Mum **(in dramatic African accent)**: *'Oh my God! I cooked for you, I cleaned for you . . . go and tell your dad!'*"

I use a very believable African accent as the voice of my mum, which my audiences actually find quite funny. It also helps me characterise my mum, again putting the audience right in the scene with me.

"*Maybe you're here today because you're trapped in a tunnel; maybe you've lost your confidence; maybe you've lost your job or a loved one and it's dark and it's cold, and you're hurting.*"

I am very soft-toned here. I make eye contact with audience members. This is one of the most import parts of my speech, and the low tone and volume of my voice expresses my own awe at my message. It also makes the audience listen harder to hear what I'm saying. I hope that I am touching lives after just sharing my own life story.

## Gestures and body language

It is a well-known fact that the majority of our communication involves body language. Eye contact, crossed arms, casual stance, hugging, hi-fives, clapping, and smiling are examples of common body language. Gestures are a deliberate form of body language communication. A speaker uses gestures and body language to enhance his message.

There is no use in smiling when you say, "I lost my job." This could lead to a miscommunication between you and your audience. It is important to use the correct gesture for the correct words and, as mentioned earlier, simple gestures can also be used to describe your characters.

### My gestures

*"I got up, wiped away the blood and his spit, and I kept on walking."*

When I make this statement, I use my hands to demonstrate wiping away the blood and spit. I repeat this gesture whenever I mention that I got up.

## Acting

Acting can help your delivery by bringing your speech to life. Acting can include many of the tools we've already discussed, including props, gestures, vocal variety and characters. There are times you may want to stand and stay planted, and other times you may want to act out a portion of your speech. Acting should only be used to bring your speech alive, if it's necessary. Too much can take away from your words and message.

> **"Acting should only be used to bring your speech alive, if it's necessary. Too much can take away from your words and message."**

### My acting

*"And on the third day, it was time for P.E. and I had to take my blazer off.* **(take off blazer and drop bag)** *"*

I literally acted out this portion of my speech, taking off my blazer and dropping my bag. Carefully choose which scenes are best to re-enact in your speech.

*"(turn to Dad) 'Dad, here are my results . . .'"*

**"Dad** (snatches paper; responds in strong African accent)*: 'My son, you are silly, you are stupid and you are slothful; get out of my sight!'"*

I act like and become my dad here, transporting my audience right into the scene.

# An inspirational ending

The concluding segment of a speech is the time when a speaker starts to leave his message and make his point. An inspirational ending is one where your audience feels like they can be, do or have more after hearing you speak. The best speakers communicate this through their vocal variety, eye contact and body movement (more on inspiring in Chapter 5).

### My inspirational ending

*"There is nothing you can't become or overcome if you keep on walking. You see our tunnels make us, our tunnels mould us, our tunnels help us realise our potential for greatness . . ."*

When I make this statement I stop telling my story and start telling my audience what they can become.

# The benefits

Always clearly explain the benefits of your message. For example, if you keep on walking, you'll see the light at the end of the tunnel. The benefits are often described in the conclusion of a speech.

### My benefits

*"Walking through my tunnels, I have become an author; walking through my tunnels I have become a football coach; walking through my tunnels I have become a speaker, because now I have things to say."*

In my conclusion, I show the benefits of walking through troubled times. Instead of sharing my whole life story, I use the rule of three to make it concise and easily relatable. I also utilise vocal variety, speaking at a fast pace to convey the message of overcoming problems.

## Unify the audience

Unifying the audience is an effective way of building rapport with your audience members. It enhances your message and creates a cooperative environment for your delivery. There are several ways to unify your audience. One way is to use collective pronouns such as "our", "us" and "we". Another way is to have your audience actually participate in your delivery, such as getting them to sing a familiar song or maybe repeating a phrase after you.

> "Unifying the audience is an effective way of building rapport with your audience members. It enhances your message and creates a cooperative environment for your delivery."

### My audience unification

*"You see **our** tunnels make **us**, **our** tunnels mould **us**, **our** tunnels help **us** realise **our** potential for greatness."*

Using "our" and "us" helps me unify my audience here as we all have struggles and can identify with each other's problems.

## The call to action

The call to action is a striking question or phrase that challenges the audience to take action based on your message.

### My call to action

*"When life throws its worst at you, you only have two choices. What will you decide? To stay trapped in a tunnel or to keep on walking?"*

I call my audience to action with a question, leaving them with a (hopefully obvious) choice.

## The call back

The call back is a reference to something previously mentioned in a speech to emphasise a thought or message, or to be humorous. Call backs help speakers conclude easily and are a creative way of telling the audience that you are wrapping up without saying "in conclusion".

### My call back

*"You see, I didn't let racism ruin me, I kept on walking; I didn't let bullying beat me, I kept on walking; I didn't let neglect knock me out, I kept on walking."*

I sum up the previous events in my speech with a call back to emphasise my message.

## Full circle technique

When a speaker starts a speech and ends a speech in the same manner, they have used the full circle technique.

### My full circle technique

*"When life throws its worst at you, you only have two choices. What will you decide? To stay trapped in a tunnel or to keep on walking?"*

I come full circle by finishing with a question that is related to my opening statement. David Sellman, a Toastmaster friend, suggested I use the full circle technique in my conclusion, and I believe it worked well to conclude my speech.

## International translation

Different regions have different rules and social norms. I learned this early in my relationship with Jim Key: when I sent him a draft script, there were words and places that he couldn't understand or weren't easily relatable to his American experience. So I had to replace a few words to make the speech more accessible to an American audience.

> Consider social norms when you're speaking internationally — some cultures may enjoy humour or entertainment, whereas other cultures may find the same humour inappropriate in public speaking."

Also consider social norms: some cultures may enjoy humour or entertainment, whereas other cultures may find the same humour inappropriate in public speaking. Be aware and remember to adapt your speech if you're speaking away from home.

### My international translation

*"I came out of Bermondsey station, walked pass the bus stop and peered into the tunnel."*

When I spoke in America, I left out the reference to "Bermondsey station", because Bermondsey had no relevance to the audience members. It wouldn't add to their overall visualisation of the scene. Instead, I simply said, "I came out of the station."

## Your turn . . .

Now that you have a summary of the techniques I have learned and used in my winning speeches, you can try and implement them in your next speech. Remember, there is no such thing as a perfect speech but a *great* speech is very attainable.

# PART 2
## WINNING FORMULAS

A formula is something that can be repeated time and time again
and yet yield the same results.

In this section you will learn my formula for speaking in 7 minutes, my formula
for writing winning speech titles, and the 2009 World Champion of Public
Speaking finalist Maureen Burns Zappala's formula for growing as a speaker.

# CHAPTER 5:

## THE 7 MINUTE FORMULA

7 minutes is a short length of time. Nowadays, audiences have shorter attention spans so as a successful speaker you need to learn how to get to your point quickly while keeping your audience engaged.

If you're a Toastmaster, 7 minutes is also the time you'll have if you enter a Toastmasters International Speech Contest. At the 7 minute mark, the judge's red light will come on, and you'll have to wrap up; if you go over 7 minutes and 30 seconds, you will be immediately disqualified.

### The bumpy bus

Beyond the rules though, the truth is that if you haven't made an impression in the first 7 minutes, you will not win it in the last 30 seconds. Think of a bus journey: if the bus ride is bumpy and uncomfortable, passengers will — given the option — get off and get another bus. If the majority of your speech is bumpy, your audience will depart way before you get to your last stop so you literally have 7 minutes to win it!

> "If you can successfully *impact*, *ignite* and *inspire* when you speak, you will have a lasting effect on your audience."

Through the process of crafting my speech and listening to many speeches, I have discovered a pattern for great speeches — I call this my 7 minute formula, and it is as easy as 1-2-3: *impact, ignite* and *inspire*. If you can successfully deliver these three actions when you speak, you will have a lasting effect on your audience, long after you've delivered your speech.

## Impact

Have you ever seen a three-minute trailer for a film and immediately thought, "I don't want to watch that!"? In a 7 minute speech, the first few words that come out of your mouth are your "trailer". Your audience will either want to listen when you talk or want to leave – your introduction is that important.

When I led a public speaking workshop in late 2011, I asked the attendees, "What is the best way to start a speech?" Answers floated from around the room: "Just say 'hello'," "Tell them your name", "Say 'thank you for clapping'." I told them in the nicest way possible that those clichéd introductions bore the audience.

As a speaker, it is important to make an instant impact – gone are the days when you could get away with starting with, "Hello, my name is . . ." Your audience don't really care what your name is, and chances are the announcer has already informed them of that detail anyway.

> "As a speaker, it is important to make an instant impact – gone are the days when you could get away with starting with, 'Hello, my name is . . .'"

So the attendees then asked me, "What is the best way to start a speech?" I replied, "Start with S.P.I.C.E." – a recipe I learned from my mum.

## Start with S.P.I.C.E.

My mum is a chef – a quality chef; I'm talking mouth-watering, "I-want-seconds!" type of cooking. The type of food you can't stop eating until you're beyond full or forced to steal from your little brother's plate when he's not looking! She makes finger-licking chicken, well-seasoned rice and fantastic fried fish, drizzled with peppers and onions marinated in olive oil and lemon juice.

One of the ingredients my mum never leaves out of her cooking is *spice* – she considers it a sin for food not to be spicy! "The spice gives the food the life," she says in her African accent, encouraging me to eat up, while I wipe the sweat from my forehead – yes, it is *that* hot!

My mum's principle doesn't just work on the plate, it also works on the platform – spice gives a speech its life. It's the magic ingredient to get a speech rolling. The best speakers don't wait until the end of their speech to add spice, they start with spice! They understand that if they don't start well, their audience won't care how well they end.

Starting with spice is important to a speaker because it grabs the audience immediately and sets the pace and expectation for the entire speech. If you're thinking, "How do I take spice to the platform?" Here's my special S.P.I.C.E. formula that you can serve with any speech you give.

## Adding S.P.I.C.E

### S is for Story

As I mentioned before, people love stories – they are a great way to connect with an audience without sounding clichéd.

For example, instead of saying "Hello, my name is Malachi and I am a public speaking champion," a better opening would be to share a story:

> "I remember sitting in the audience in May last year waiting for the contest chairman to announce the winner of the UK and Ireland Speech Contest. And then I heard the words: 'The UK and Ireland Champion for 2011 is . . . Malachi Talabi!' That moment changed my life."

With this introduction I've just shared personal details with the audience, without sounding clichéd – just by using a story. This story introduction would grab my audience's attention; now they are curious about how and why I entered the contest, how I felt after winning, and, if they are public speakers, they may want to know what skills I developed on the way.

I've evoked interest in all these areas in a unique and original way without explicitly spelling out my intentions to do so. The key to using a story is to make sure that the story supports your speech.

> "The key to using a story is to make sure that the story supports your speech."

### P is for Pause

I never used to pause in my speeches until Phillip Khan-Panni, a silver medallist in the Toastmasters International Public Speaking Contest, taught me how to and when. Before then, I usually spoke too fast, which made it hard for my audience to understand me – that was until I learned that a pause is a very powerful and effective way to start a speech.

The pause heightens the anticipation of your audience and helps to still the atmosphere before you speak. Starting with a pause may feel awkward, but, oh boy, is it spicy! When you do this, scan the room and use eye contact to connect with your audience — it will make your presentation more personal and conversational.

### I is for Intriguing question, quote, or statistic

Questions are powerful. As I mentioned in Chapter 4, there are several different types of questions — power questions, you-focused questions, rhetorical questions, and more — which can be used to provoke a reaction from your audience. When starting with S.P.I.C.E., quotes and statistics can also have this effect.

If you stepped on the stage and asked, "Have you ever felt you could be, do and have more than you currently have?" Even if they don't verbally respond, the audience's reaction to this question could be yes, no, or maybe, tell me more!

You can use an intriguing quote instead: *"Pessimists see a doormat; optimists see a welcome mat."* This would get members of your audience thinking, "Which one am I?" Or you can shock with an intriguing statistic. "Ten thousand people will lose their jobs before the end of the month." Your audience will be exclaiming, "Wow, I can't believe that!"

The more intriguing the question, quote, or statistic, the greater the reaction you are likely to get from your audience.

### C is for Call Back

The call back is commonly used in the comedy world — it's a simple reference to something said earlier in your speech or something the audience may have heard during the event, or even in the course of the week (such as news or current affairs). Using a call back connects you with your audience and can also call to attention important messages in your speech.

To start with a call back, reference a current event or something that happened before you got on stage. For example, if

> "Using a call back connects you with your audience and can also call to attention important messages in your speech."

your audience has just finished eating ice cream before your speech, incorporate the ice cream into your introduction:

> *"It's cold outside but somehow when I tasted that delicious ice cream, I warmed right up! Maybe if we applaud and all scream for ice cream the waiters will give us seconds!"*

If the speaker before you said something funny, work that into a call back. Be creative and use something relatable for the audience as this makes the speech more intimate and, if done right, can be quite funny. In a speech contest, the call back is very entertaining and an effective tool of connection, but remember to watch the time!

### E is for Entertainment

Starting with entertainment may mean wearing or using a prop or visual aid, telling a funny (but short) story, or even using music or singing a song. Entertainment is an effective early engager because your audience members do not want to be bored, and neither do you! Entertaining early in your presentation makes the audience anticipate the rest of your speech. And you'll be more relaxed when you see the excitement on the faces of your audience.

As the host of a book launch, I started my presentation with entertainment. Afterwards, a woman approached me and said, "I thought this would be a standard boring book launch in a library, but after hearing you, I was pleasantly surprised!" I made sure I started with S.P.I.C.E. by entertaining early. In a speech contest, you must tie the entertainment into your speech, while keeping in mind that time is precious.

S.P.I.C.E. is an effective way to add impact to your public speaking. Starting with one of the five spicy appetisers – stories, pause, intrigue, call back or entertainment – ensures your audience will enjoy the whole meal. Just as my mum would never serve food without spice, I would never start a speech without S.P.I.C.E. – I guess it's in my DNA!

> **Starting with one of the five spicy appetisers – stories, pause, intrigue, call back or entertainment – ensures your audience will enjoy the whole meal.**

Always make sure that your impact supports your whole speech. I started Keep on Walking with a pause, followed by an intriguing statement which included my speech title. Utilising all of these tools made a bigger impact on my audience than a traditional "hello" or "thank you". Making an immediate impact invites your audience into your speech and allows them to anticipate what is to come.

# Ignite

You may be thinking, "Malachi, what do you mean by *ignite* your audience?" I mean set them ablaze! Start a fire that grips them and grabs them!

You should aim to ignite in the body of your speech, right after your opening impact. Just like a fire would make a room hot, your story can make your audience feel something. Tell your story in a way that stimulates a response from your audience and ignites their emotions. This is where word pictures, vocal variety and acting are extremely important and effective; In fact, they are the main tools that the best speakers use to ignite their audience.

### Ignite with words

There is a saying that actions speak louder than words. Well, in public speaking, words often speak louder than actions, if they are said at the right pace, pitch and volume.

Word pictures are powerful. They help an audience see and feel during the telling of a story. When I say, "I laid there in a pool of blood", my audience could visualise both the scene and my pain. They also might form questions in their own minds: "What did he do next?" "How did he get through that?" Taking time to vividly describe the scenes and characters is important because these are the elements of a speech that help the audience re-create their own version of your journey. I remember delivering my speech and seeing the shocked look on people's faces in some parts — some people even covered their eyes! I knew I had ignited them.

> "Taking time to vividly describe the scenes and characters is important because these are the elements of a speech that help the audience re-create their own version of your journey."

To ignite your audience your speech should include conflict and twists. These added dimensions to your story will build upon the initial impact you created.

Many of the tools outlined in Chapter 4 can also be effective igniting methods; for instance, when using characters, it is important to determine who will have a voice and how that voice will sound.

Using vocal variety can be very effective; acting out portions of your speech can also help your audience easily visualise the scene and message. If you use the correct gestures your speech will be unforgettable. In Keep on Walking, whenever I was "in the tunnel", I acted out the encounter. I knew that this, coupled with word pictures and vocal variety, would ignite my audience and have them on the edge of their seats to see and hear how the story would end.

I used these igniting techniques in the body of the speech at approximately the four and five minute marks. Mix up the tones, gestures, pauses, and other techniques to maximise the "ignite" you bring to your audience.

### Ignite with questions

Questions can not only help you impact your audience early on, they can also help you to ignite. In Keep on Walking, I ask the audience, "Has life ever thrown a punch at you that you weren't prepared for?" When I ask this question, it is my intention to ignite their emotions.

Questions can make your audience members reflect on their own lives and relate more to your story. You're taking your audience on a visual and emotional journey and your message is so important that you need to use every tool in your arsenal to evoke a response from your audience.

Word pictures, vocal variety, acting, and asking questions are all keys to igniting your audience during your speech.

# Inspire

First impressions count, and last impressions stick. I believe that the best place to inspire is at the beginning of your conclusion. You may think, "Well, that's what my whole speech was designed to do", and while that may be true, if you have impacted and ignited your audience, by the time you start your conclusion they will be even more ready for you to drive your point home.

This is the place where you can challenge your audience to think, act or become something different; this is where you can plant a powerful call to action, or leave your audience with a powerful rhetorical question.

By the conclusion of Keep on Walking, I had turned up the volume, passion and pause. I had forgotten about the contest and was focused on the crowd. This was my moment to lay all my cards on the table and sell my message to change lives. I used many tools, including power lines, the rule of three, repetition of my foundational phrase, and vocal variety, to ensure my audience members hear me, see me and feel me.

> "By inspiring in your conclusion, you can really help someone who might be on the edge of defeat or depression to overcome those low feelings."

The conclusion is often the most emotional part of a speech. By inspiring in your conclusion, you can really help someone who might be on the edge of defeat or depression to overcome those low feelings. This is the place to bring your "A-game"; it is where you can really release your emotions so use the tools and tricks at your disposal.

When inspiring your audience, there are a few things to bear in mind:

### Don't shout at your audience

I always encourage speakers to show passion on the stage but I have also learned that shouting does not inspire. Yes, raise the tone and volume of your voice occasionally; yes, show urgency through vocal variety; but be careful not to shout. This could destroy the whole tone and effect of your speech and the last thing you want to do is lose your audience at the end!

Remember that your audience has been reflecting on your story and their life circumstances, and some may even be emotionally ready to make a personal change in their thinking or behaviour. Be sensitive to your audience and their emotions in your conclusion.

You can also use the power of pause at important and poignant places to temper high emotions. Instead of projecting loudly and persistently, I have learned that sometimes a pause can be more powerful than projection. A pause draws an audience into the world of your speech.

When I have, on occasion, shouted at my audience when speaking, their facial expressions appear to be asking, "What's your problem?" Our task is public speaking, not lecturing or acting like angry school teachers.

## Paint scenarios

In your inspirational conclusion, you can also paint scenarios and ask questions. For example, if, in the body of your speech, you have told a story about overcoming financial ruin, you now have the opportunity to say, "What decisions have ruined *your* finances? Was it too much take-away food? Those extra pair of shoes? A new mobile phone?" These questions engage your audience in a relatable way. Asking questions in the conclusion helps an audience face their own personal situation and could inspire them to change.

## Practice your passion

I used to prefer not to practice or write the inspirational and passionate portions of my speeches. I felt it would be more powerful if I were spontaneous and instantly speaking from my heart, "keeping it real" on stage. Then I discovered that my realness was actually rawness, and it turned off the majority of my audience. My solution from then became to always practice my passion before the platform!

> "The key to delivering passionate portions of your speech is to practice and record your practice."

The key to delivering passionate portions of your speech is to practice and record your practice. Recording and reviewing yourself changes your perspective from speaker to audience member and allows you to truly see yourself as your audience would.

Finally, having an inspirational ending is important in speech contests or any other presentation – your ending is the very last words and emotions you leave with your audience so leave them with a treat.

So there you have it – the 7 minute formula! This is not necessarily a specific guide to the perfect speech, rather it is a template to help you deliver a memorable message. In Part 4, you will read winning speeches from champions, some of which adapt these principles and others that don't. The key is to take what works with you and adapt it to your speaking style the next time you have the opportunity to take the stage.

# CHAPTER 6:

## STORIES AND THE EMOTIONAL JOURNEY

Can you remember tales from your childhood, like "Little Red Riding Hood", "Goldilocks and the Three Bears", or "The Three Little Pigs"? Most likely you can because they are *stories*.

I have had about five mobile phone numbers over the last few years and I can't remember any of them off the top of my head, nor can I remember all the numbers stored in my phone. I can, however, recall details from childhood stories easier than I can recall phone numbers I dialled last week! The last time I heard Little Red Riding Hood was over 20 years ago but I can vividly remember every character's full lines of dialogue.

Stories are easy to remember because they touch the heart, mind and soul. Stories are easily relatable and entertaining and for this reason, audiences will choose to listen to and remember a story over a statistic any day. For you as a public speaker, stories lead to glory.

> "Stories are easy to remember because they touch the heart, mind and soul."

### Tell a story or give a lecture?

Growing up, the one thing I couldn't stand was a lecture. As a typical teen, I played "knock down ginger" (knocking on doors and running away), took biscuits from the tin in the kitchen when I shouldn't, and went to bed way past my bed time – that meant that I lived in "Lecture City".

My mum would lecture me, my aunty would lecture me, my teachers and professors would lecture me, the preacher at church would lecture me, and when I got married, my wife decided to join the lecture club too! The only way I could survive Lecture City was to visit "Wonderland".

Wonderland is where I travelled when my mum, dad, school teacher or preacher began their lectures. I got so good at escaping to Wonderland that I mastered the art of looking interested while someone spoke. I would nod at the right places, finish the right phrases, and even put on the sprinklers when necessary, mastering the art of "crocodile tears"! All the while, I was thinking about the football I would play, the girls I would meet, and the food I would eat once I got out of Lecture City.

If you don't want your audience to visit Wonderland when you speak, don't take them to Lecture City, lead them to "Storyville" instead! Engage your audience in your speech for the whole 7 minutes that you have their attention and there's no better way to do this than to wrap your principles and messages into a story. While they are in Storyville, you can be changing their lives.

## Here's why you should tell a story

We've already established that stories are easier to remember than unembellished statistics or statements. I can't recall the strategic marketing plans that my university professor tried to teach me through a lecture, but I wonder what would have happened if he had wrapped his teaching into a story — maybe I would have remembered his lessons and got better grades!

Stories are great because they teach without preaching, allowing your audience to make up their own minds without feeling the pressure and unhappiness of a trip to Lecture City. Stories help you to appear less judgemental and critical, even if you have some tough content to deliver. We grow up listening to stories, whether it is through fairytales, movies, books or magazines. We live in a society that teaches and instructs through stories so why reinvent the wheel?

> **"We live in a society that teaches and instructs through stories so why reinvent the wheel?"**

## Choose your story

There are many types of stories to tell – fairy tales, comedies, myths and fables, historical stories and much more. The world is your oyster full of pearls of stories!

When I competed in the International Speech Contest, personal stories were the most popular type of stories I came across and the higher the round, the more personal the stories. At the same time, I have heard successful contest speeches which feature historical and cultural stories of triumph and overcoming obstacles. I have also heard speeches about Martin Luther King Jr. and other famous figures past and present, as well as humorous stories based on life's funny little situations – all these have done well in contests.

Don't limit yourself to one particular type of story – whatever story format effectively carries your message is the best one to tell. Personal stories work well because they help to connect you as a speaker to your audience. They are also easier to remember and they allow you to protect your uniqueness – no matter how similar your story is to someone else's, no one has lived your exact unique life. Telling other people's stories is okay but when you tell other people's stories, you run the risk of another speaker having the same basic material as you so just ensure you personalise it by telling it in your own words.

## 7 minutes, several emotions . . .

Have you considered that if you speak about subjects like death or loss, your audience will be likely to empathise with you and reflect on similar experiences in their own lives? Similarly, if you speak about a funny situation, your audience will experience feelings of joy and happiness.

> "Every story has a set of emotions attached to it. When you speak in public you are taking your audience on an emotional journey."

In the minute-by-minute analysis of Keep on Walking, you may notice that there is only one place reserved for a laugh, during the fourth minute. I didn't perceive that as a problem until I sought Jim Key's advice after the district contest and he said: "Your speech is good, but it's very intense – it could do with a little more humour."

Another Toastmaster also commented at the time, "I loved your speech, but it made me feel sad." I wanted to have an impact on my audience, but I didn't want to leave them feeling down and depressed! I didn't yet realise that every story has a set of emotions attached to it. When you speak in public you are taking your audience on an emotional journey.

## The emotional journey

You cannot dictate the emotions of your audience, nor should you try to either, but understanding what emotions are attached to your stories can ensure you deliver a more effective speech. You only have 7 minutes to win it – if you take your audience member's emotions too low, you may not have enough time to bring them back up.

If we graph the emotional journey of Keep on Walking, it would look something like this:

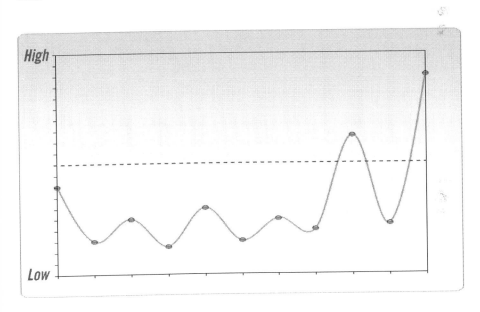

As I share stories from my childhood that involve bullying and neglect, my audience spend a lot of time on the downside of the emotional journey and then about halfway through, the humour comes in to bring them to an upswing. As Jim was trying to point out, the injection of humour lifts the audience from the lowest point. I then continue to raise my audience's emotions towards the inspiring ending. In reflection, there is still room for improvement – places where I could inject a bit more humour into the speech and still deliver my serious message.

Although continuing with my usual speech pattern (not using much humour) worked for me in the UK and Ireland Speech Contest, Jim's words led me on a search for humour. I knew that my speech was too intense and I didn't want this to cloud my message.

I uncovered humour in the speech by giving my audience permission to laugh. Jim taught me that adding a smile where my audience may want to laugh but might be reluctant to do so because of a serious subject, is a good way to release tension and intensity. Phrases like, "It's okay to laugh", or "I laugh at it, too", or "I can laugh about it now", delivered with a smile, make the audience feel more comfortable. I believe that making this slight adjustment greatly enhanced my speech. I received many more laughs in the semi-final round in Las Vegas.

### Scott's speech

The contestant who won my segment of the semi-finals was Scott Pritchard, a stand-up comedian and show host. He delivered an extremely funny speech which was also surprisingly touching and really special. His speech was called *1980: A Touch Can Do So Much* and it was based on a school friend who died. It had plenty of humour and a big unexpected twist.

The emotional journey on which Scott took his audience was extremely powerful. If you graphed the journey, it would look something like this:

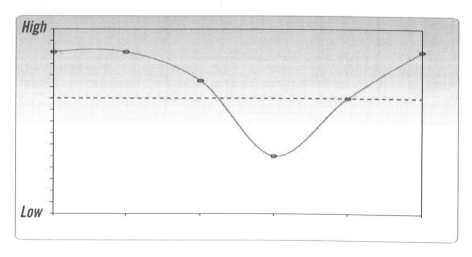

Scott started his speech with a lot of humour – he was so funny that I thought he was in the wrong contest! He immediately connected with the audience through his characters, and then suddenly there was a big twist – someone dies and the abrupt and unexpected leap from joy to sorrow led to an instant sobering moment.

> "Balancing the highs and lows in your speech is extremely important – you don't want your audience to leave your speech having nightmares!"

By the end of his speech however, Scott brought us back up to the previous emotional high with a very strong ending and finished third place in the world finals (you can read Scott's speech in Part 4 and listen to it on the *7 Minute Champions* audio).

I learned that humour can really build rapport between a speaker and their audience. Balancing the highs and lows in your speech is extremely important – you don't want your audience to leave your speech having nightmares! Knowing the emotions that your speech evokes can help you structure your speech and evaluate if you are communicating emotions that support your message. Receiving evaluations of your speech, including self-evaluations of recorded practice, will help with this process (see Chapter 11 for more on evaluations).

## Tips to remember on your emotional journey

### 1) Flat is bad

If your speech is void of emotions you are unlikely to have a big impact on your audience. People are moved by emotion and an emotion-packed speech will engage your audience. Choose your stories wisely and anticipate possible audience reactions.

Similarly, your speech shouldn't be flat by being just one emotion throughout (unless it is intended as a humorous speech). Having just sad or depressing material can drag your audience down; release the tension with a bit of humour, but remember that being overly humorous in an inspirational speech may distract your audience from your main message.

Balance and contrast is key but whatever you do, make sure your speech is not flat!

### 2) Take them up the mountain, not on a rollercoaster

When climbing a mountain you experience both lows and highs but the journey is all worth it if you end up on top.

Scott and I both ended our speeches on high emotional points, leaving our audiences with good feelings. In general, people like happy endings, especially if they feel like they've climbed a mountain to get there.

A rollercoaster is the exact opposite of a steady climb of emotions. A rollercoaster speech is one that has too many emotions moving too quickly – fear, joy, pain, loss, regret and excitement, all in the same 7 minutes! This can be too much for most audience members to process in 7 minutes and can make a message seem disjointed.

> "A rollercoaster speech is one that has too many emotions moving too quickly – fear, joy, pain, loss, regret and excitement, all in the same 7 minutes!"

Your stories and the emotions they carry must match the message you deliver – save the rollercoaster for a keynote speech where you have more time. Nine times out of ten, it's best to end on a high!

### 3) The plus-minus technique

In her book Using Stories and Humour (Essence of Public Speaking), Joanna Slan says, "Once you put together an entire presentation, you should graph the emotional highs and lows."

She suggests creating an outline of your presentation then down the side of the page, adding plus signs for highs and upbeat moments and minus signs for downbeat sections. After this analyse the whole pattern, keeping in mind that audiences can't sustain feelings of sadness and unhappiness for too long. Always make sure you have some humour and hope.

It is important to know the emotions that your speech carries so that your audience really gets the heart of your message.

# CHAPTER 7:

## KNOW, GROW AND GO

In the next section of the book we will look at how you can start writing your own 7 minute masterpiece. But first, I want to share with you speaking advice from a lady who is a real champion in many ways.

During my trip to Las Vegas, I met speaker and coach Maureen Burns Zappala, who has since become my friend and speaking mentor. Maureen has had the privilege of learning from some of the best public speaking champions, and she even placed in the top ten of over 25,000 contestants at the Toastmasters International Speech Contest world finals in 2009. Maureen kindly agreed to share some tips that will help shorten your learning curve as a speaker.

## Maureen's three tips to winning

If you walked in to my NASA office one day in the mid-90s where I managed a jet engine research facility in Cleveland, Ohio, you would have seen me slumped in my chair, drowning in discouragement. I had just given a crucial presentation — you know the type, the one that can make or break your career. My boss, a man I respected and admired, gave me some devastating news. He said, "Maureen, you are a really bad speaker."

It was true! I *was* bad! My skills, my confidence, my effectiveness — all were really bad. So, how did I go from a woman who tortured her audiences to a woman who was privileged to stand on stage, speak to 2,000 people, and compete for the title of the World Champion of Public Speaking? A lot changed, didn't it? My journey to the World Championship was magical and memorable, but it was also methodical — I had focus and purpose.

The truths I learned on my journey are ones that you can use on yours. There's nothing unique about me. To quote 2005 World Champion Lance Miller, "I am just a product of Toastmasters." I'm convinced that Toastmasters works, but only if YOU do. And if I can do it, you can too!

> "In the 14 weeks between the District 10 contest and the International finals, I was transformed both as a speaker and a person."

In the 14 weeks between the District 10 contest and the International finals, I was transformed both as a speaker and a person. To summarise, the one colossal and significant truth I learned is this: you can't do it alone. Shocking, huh? But that truth manifested itself in three aspects.

### 1) You can't know it alone, you need education

Have you heard the saying "good speakers are made, not born"? It's true, I'm living proof! Skills do not come from the inside, they come from the outside, and you put them inside. But I didn't know that! I thought I was a pretty good speaker, after all, heading into the contest season in the spring of 2009 and having been in Toastmasters for about 6 years, I had already won over 35 contests. But I really was clueless.

When I won the District contest in May 2009, I was thrilled! It was my dream to advance to the regional, and now I did it! As I faced the regional contest, a casual conversation with a past District Governor was my first clue that I was indeed clueless about speechwriting. No longer could I advance on charm and energy. I needed to learn real speaking skills. I began an educational odyssey that opened my eyes to a universe of tools to help me grow.

A Toastmaster friend loaned me some CDs and DVD recordings of educational sessions at past conventions. Distinguished Toastmaster Jamey French, a man I had never met but to whom I was connected through a mutual friend, loaned me his entire collection of past World Championship contest DVDs, hundreds of dollars of his investment for hours of contest speeches. His generosity touched the deepest part of my heart. I poured over that material and soaked up every bit of information I could.

I was humbled by how little I knew about speechwriting. I became a serious student of public speaking. I learned how to connect with an audience, how to tell an effective story, how to create a gripping word picture, and how to use the power of the pause. I read books on public speaking, scoured the internet for resources and articles, and absorbed any lessons I could. Do not overlook the colossal amount of information available both inside and outside Toastmasters. You need to know what you don't know.

> "Do not overlook the colossal amount of information available both inside and outside Toastmasters. You need to know what you don't know."

## 2) You can't grow it alone – you need coaching

Have you ever received an evaluation that wasn't very useful? Unfortunately, many evaluations from well-meaning Toastmasters are not specific enough, not informative enough, and sometimes not truthful enough. To grow your skills, you don't need just an evaluation, you need a coach – someone who has been where you want to go, who will interact with you in real time, and who will tell you what you need to hear, not just what you want to hear.

While I prepared for the Regional, my fellow club member, David Caban, gave me some of the most valuable and extensive feedback I ever heard. He walked this road before. In 1999, he took third place in the World Championship finals, so he knew what he was talking about. I picked his brain for every tidbit of information he had. I made a pest of myself. I called him, emailed him and sucked up all his time after meetings. I hung on every word he said because he observed things that never occurred to me. His evaluations were honest, specific and gentle. And they were exactly what I needed.

When I won the Regional contest in June 2009, people told me, "Call the World Champions . . . they'll help coach you!" Well, that was completely intimidating to me! These people were the icons of the speaker training industry, almost unapproachable to me. I'm just a stay-at-home mom . . . how could they rub shoulders with me?

But I kept hearing it over and over. "Call the champions. Call them!" I finally harvested the courage to call Darren LaCroix. He didn't answer, so I left a message. Within 45 minutes, he called back. When the phone rang, I answered "Hello?" I heard Darren's familiar voice (having spent hours watching past championship speeches on DVD!) He exclaimed, "Is this THE Maureen Zappala? The famous Region 6 champion?" He was genuinely excited about my win. I found the same thing with the other champions that I contacted. I ended up working closely with Jim Key, Darren LaCroix and past finalist Rory Vaden . . . all three of them were committed not to my win, but to my growth. They live to give.

Working with coaches is humbling and hard. You must be teachable, coachable and trainable. Darren LaCroix, often asks, "Do you want education or validation?" I didn't want just a pat on the head and "Good job, Maureen". I needed significant adjustments in my speaking skills, and these men gave it to me . . . in HUGE doses!

> "Working with coaches is humbling and hard. You must be teachable, coachable and trainable."

My coaches helped me in three areas:

1.  Brevity is not my gift. I'm wordy. They challenged me to raise my wordsmithing to a completely different level. Did you know that most people write a nine minute speech and try to deliver it in 7 minutes? The champs write a five minute speech and deliver it in six. My final speech was much more precise and concise (735 words) because of their coaching. I've heard it said by many of the champs, "A great speech is not written. It is rewritten."

2.  The journey to the World Championship of Public Speaking is an emotional and physical rollercoaster that often knocked me off my track. I laughed. I cried. I groused. Yet, I could count on my coaches to recalibrate my anxiety and get my wobbly wheels back on track. They believed in me and helped me believe in myself.

3.  I was weak in staging. How many of us speak from such a huge platform? I needed specific help to use the stage to my greatest advantage. Darren LaCroix spent hours with me at the convention to work on staging. I have a habit of pacing. During a practice session, he got down on the ground and held my ankles and said, "OKAY, now speak." He transformed the visual impact of my speech just by making me aware of my position on the stage.

While there was a tremendous amount of information those coaches gave me, there were some significant pieces that every one of us can use for every one of our speeches:

1. **Your message MUST resonate with you!** Mark Hunter, the 2009 World Champion, said about his message, "It's one that I both love and live. If you don't love it and live it, you cannot give it." My message was so much a part of me that it was so much easier to deliver. Give a message that is *consistent* with who you are, so that it *flows* from who you are.

2. **SLOW DOWN!** Your pacing is crucial. If you simply slow down, add longer pauses, and wait for the audience, you'll be amazed at their response.

3. **Quoting Darren LaCroix: "STAGE TIME! STAGE TIME! STAGE TIME!"** Practice as much as you can in front of a live audience. Not in front of a mirror, or in an empty room, but in front of live people. For the finals, I practiced at 22 Toastmasters clubs and events.

4. **Record every practice session . . . and then WATCH the recording!** It will be painful. But it's the quickest way to get better. When you see yourself on video, you see what works and what doesn't. You need to see what the audience gets to see!

### 3) You can't go it alone – you need support

Isn't Toastmasters filled with fascinating people? The fact is, although I didn't win the contest, I still feel like a winner, because my prize wasn't the trophy, it was the relationships I developed along the way. So many people poured into my life to make this journey amazing. I enjoyed the journey because they joined the journey.

The support from my region and my District 10 was precious. They lifted me and propelled me. All the notes, emails, phone calls and words of encouragement I received invigorated and inspired me, and I am deeply grateful for that. Mark Hunter, said, "It takes a club to raise a member, but it takes a District to raise a champion."

At the convention, I enjoyed celebrity treatment. My coaches made me feel like royalty. My International Director, Kristal DiCarlo, made it a point to introduce me to as many people as she knew. And as an ID, she knows a lot of people. I revelled in her shadow and enjoyed a piece of her spotlight. I met past finalists, other World Champions, District Governors and International Directors. I mingled with Toastmasters from all over the world. In a nutshell, I schmoozed with as many people as I could.

While it was fun, it was for a reason. I confess: as a speaker, I am intimidated to address a crowd of strangers. I need to connect with individuals first. By the time I took the stage on Saturday morning to speak to 2,000 people, I bet I had met 200 of them. I no longer was speaking to strangers. I was speaking to friends. And that made all the difference in the world. Make the effort to meet and greet your audience before you speak, and for you too it will make all the difference in the world.

> "Make the effort to meet and greet your audience before you speak, and for you too it will make all the difference in the world."

The day before the contest, I met the other contestants in the briefing, and the camaraderie was electric. While it was clear there was intensity in the room, we were celebrating just getting there! There was a mutual respect . . . we all knew the work it took to get there. I enjoyed being with so many other accomplished speakers. I wasn't competing against them. I was competing with them.

The contest exceeded all my expectations for fun and fanfare, and in my mind, the judges got it right. Champion Mark Hunter is not only an extraordinary communicator, he's an extraordinary person, well suited as a fine ambassador for Toastmasters. It's my pleasure and honour to know him.

It was a momentous chapter in life. Having been challenged, changed and cheered, the experience is a milestone for me, a defining era. I may be without a trophy, but I am not without a treasure, for the greater value is found in the lessons I learned, not the applause I heard. I was once a "really bad speaker", but now I'm a really blessed woman. And if I can do it, so can you.

---

Now that you know the power of coaching, I would like to invite you to join me in the Champions' Corner – my interactive coaching resource centre. Just go to http://resources.malachitalabi.com

# PART 3:
## YOUR 7 MINUTE MASTERPIECE

Now that you've learnt the techniques, gone behind the scenes of a winning 7 minute speech, and heard from a champion, it's time for you to create your own 7 minute masterpiece.

*"The best speeches are not written, they are re-written"*

— Darren LaCroix —

# CHAPTER 8:

## WRITING YOUR 7 MINUTE MASTERPIECE

*"How will I find my story? What will I speak about? This is not going to be easy!"*

These were my initial thoughts when I sat down to write my speech for the International Speech Contest. I was panicking – I didn't have it all together but I ended up winning so don't worry if you start with similar questions!

Below, I've included a basic outline that most speeches follow. Use this outline, and the questions, tips, and selected readings as a guide when you set pen to paper. Once you have answered the questions and reviewed the relevant chapters, the river of ideas will start to flow!

Remember, this is just an exercise to start sketching out your speech – it doesn't need to be perfect.

### What's your objective?

The first thing you must determine before you begin to write your speech is your objective – what do you want to accomplish? There are usually four objectives that a speech is based around: inspiration, persuasion, information or entertainment. Sometimes the four main objectives may overlap (for example, you can persuade and entertain at the same time), but usually there is only one main objective. Whenever you give a speech, even

> **"Whenever you give a speech, even if you don't know what you are going to share, at least aim to know your objective."**

if you don't know what you are going to share, at least aim to know your objective.

The next thing that you must decide upon is your subject. What will you talk about? I heard a man give an inspirational speech about avocados in the second round of my contest. He had a clear objective – to inspire – and he had his subject – avocados. He was very clear and this communicated a sense of purpose to the audience. If your objective is to persuade, your subject could be football and your message could be "footballers should act as role models".

Setting your objective and subject early will help you have more clarity when searching for your message and stories. My objective in Keep on Walking was to inspire and my subject was overcoming adversity – you can literally choose to write about any subject you want, whether it is breaking habits, decision making, discipline, overcoming fear, personal growth, health and wellbeing, positive thinking, self-respect and so on.

## Finding your message

Once your objective and subject are set, you can step into the creative process of choosing your stories and finding your message.

When I entered the International Speech Contest, I had my objective and subject (I got it from the Toastmaster manual as this was a speech task), however I was lacking the stories and illustrations to put my speech together. I still couldn't find an inspirational message. I knew I was going to inspire my audience, and I knew I wouldn't be telling any knock-knock jokes, but I was frustrated. I asked myself questions and did a lot of reflecting in that time and waited for "the big message" to come. I was very lucky that waiting paid off and my message eventually came through writing down personal stories on scraps of paper. It's very empowering when this happens, but the difficult thing can be waiting for it to happen.

What I learnt was that waiting can be very risky, especially when you have a deadline. Sometimes getting a plain piece of paper and just writing down your thoughts, doing a mind map, or writing out a personal story can help unlock your creativity. You may find that thousands of ideas start to

> "Sometimes getting a plain piece of paper and just writing down your thoughts, doing a mind map, or writing out a personal story can help unlock your creativity."

come to mind. You may just want to try sitting down and writing what happened in your day and add that to your ideas without having a strict message set out in stone. This was my writing style. I literally just started writing, and then it all seemed to come together – my speech title, my phrases, even ideas for gestures I would use.

Now before I write, I usually *try* to figure out my message before I find my story or illustration. This is less risky and more systematic because it doesn't mean leaving it up to fate any more. Sometimes waiting for an idea to drop out of the sky means you'll be writing your speech two minutes before you take the stage. I find that determining my message first also helps me to write faster and triggers thoughts and stories that will support my message.

Here are some questions to help you find your message once you have your objective and subject:

- Who are my audience?

- What do I want my audience to think, believe, or do differently as a result of my speech?

If, for example, my objective is to inspire, my subject is healthy eating and my audience members are women, I may decide that what I want them to do after hearing my speech is to eat more fruits and vegetables. In that case, my message may be, "Eat more fruits and vegetables so you can live longer, look younger and wear whatever you want!"

Once you have a message, you must select the best method to share it – this could be personal stories, historical stories, cultural stories, analogies or news stories.

## Gathering your stories

The next step is to gather your stories. At this stage I would search for examples in my life, in newspapers, on the news or in books that will support my message and inspire my audience to think and act differently.

> "Whichever way you find your objective, subject, message and stories, it's important to make sure that your message is relevant and compelling."

Sometimes I find that once I have my message I tend to find that I can immediately think of parts of my life or metaphors or illustrations I've come across that can support the message. This method works well because as soon as you've chosen your message, your mind will usually get to work to help you find your stories.

Whichever way you find your objective, subject, message and stories, it's important to make sure that your message is relevant and compelling.

## The bare bones

Now that you have your objective, subject, message and stories, it's time to sketch out the "bare bones" – a skeleton of your entire speech in only five or six lines.

Using Keep on Walking as a base, I can put together a new speech with these bare bones:

> "When I was younger, my dad was in Nigeria and we were extremely poor. I found it hard to go to school for even one day without being bullied. I even suffered a racist attack! When I got to college, things brightened up, until I got my results and my dad got a hold of them. In fact, both my parents were disappointed. I felt so depressed in that period of my life, but I walked through it. Since then, I have written books, won speaking contests and become a football coach, all because I kept on going."

Write out the bare bones of your speech, bearing in mind your objective and subject. Once this is ready, you can now add the 7 minute formula to impact, ignite and inspire!

## Your speech title

Your speech title may evolve naturally as you write – it may be a foundational phrase or it may utilise one of the "Four T's of a Tantalising Title" which we'll talk about in the next chapter.

If I had a speech title for the bare bones above, it would be either "You are worth it" or "Are you worth it?" because the message is about restoring self-worth.

## Your introduction

So you now have your bare bones and your speech title, the next thing to consider is which S.P.I.C.E. ingredient you want to use to start your speech. Remember, you are now adding "meat" to the bones.

In your introduction, it is important to establish a setting by answering who, what, where, when and why. So my bare bones introduction is:

> "When I was younger my dad was in Nigeria and we were extremely poor . . ."

> "In your introduction, it is important to establish a setting by answering who, what, where, when and why."

Using the S.P.I.C.E. principle, I can now add meat to these bones by starting with a story:

> "I was 10 years old, my dad was in Nigeria and whenever I asked my mum for pocket money, she would say, "Do I look like a bank? I walk to work – how do you expect to get pocket money?"

I've started with a story and I've chosen a part of the bare bones to expand, adding dialogue and specifics such as my age.

Choose which S.P.I.C.E. ingredient you want to use in your speech – practice "fleshing" out your introduction with a story. Consider these questions:

- Who are my main characters?

- How will I establish them early in the introduction?

- How will I transition from the introduction to the body?

## Building your characters

Characters are important to any story because audiences can easily relate to a well-developed character. It's important that your audience can visualise your characters therefore how you present them directly impacts their ability to do this.

I have found that sometimes characters like a wife or a mum do not need a detailed description because, for the most part, the audience can envisage these characters. The only time your audience needs a detailed description of a character is when they provide a major outcome in your story.

> "The only time your audience needs a detailed description of a character is when they provide a major outcome in your story."

Effective character development can heighten the suspense and conflict in a speech. For example, I could start a speech by saying: "The bully came into the classroom . . ." To be more effective however, I could start with:

> *"He was six-foot-two and his muscles rippled as the class bully strode into the classroom with a devilish grin . . ."*

This more complete description and characterisation immediately heightens the tension and paints a very clear mental picture. The difficulty is to find a good balance: paint a good picture, but don't go overboard with your descriptions and details.

Sometimes the length of the story and the role of the character are good determining factors in finding the balance between too much or too little character development. You must use your best judgement, and that is when evaluations and experience come in handy.

When building your character, consider the following questions:

- What is my character's height and/or weight?

- How old are they?

- What is their gender?

- What is their racial background?

- Is there a celebrity they look like?

- What is their religious background?

- What is their occupation?

- What metaphor can I use to describe their characteristic? (For example, their voice sounds like . . . they laugh like this . . .)

Once you have this information it will help you decide how you introduce your character or characters, what lines of dialogue to inject into your speech, and what parts of your speech you may wish to act out.

## Filling out the body

Now look at your bare bones outline and consider how you want to move your story along. In the introduction, you would have established the setting, the characters, and the conflict, now it's time to ignite your audience. As you tell your story, use vocal variety, acting and word pictures to draw your audience in and ignite their emotional journey. Here's the body of my example speech:

> *"I was 10 years old, my dad was in Nigeria, and whenever I asked my mum for pocket money she would say, "Do I look like a bank? I walk to work — how do you expect to get pocket money?"*

> *After years of being bullied and that incident with Terry, I was scarred emotionally. I would look in the mirror and think, "You are worthless." Every time I failed a school test, I would say, "You are worthless." If you could see a picture of how I felt, you would see a shipwreck — the pieces of wood represent the broken parts of my life. I felt like nothing. My bullies had stolen everything precious: my self-worth, my pride, and my confidence, and I woke up feeling empty, worried and worthless.*

> *Have you ever been shipwrecked? Have the pirates ever plundered anything precious from you? What made matters worse for me was that I wanted comfort, but as a teenager, comfort means girlfriend! It was hard to find a girlfriend — the odds were stacked against me: first of all, I went to an all-boys school, and secondly, no money meant I couldn't afford even a cinema ticket and girls expected guys to pay — my wife still does; some things never change!"*

In this body I've asked a you-focused question, used a metaphor and described word pictures to build the meat and start igniting my audience. Remember, your story is for your audience and your questions give them the opportunity to reflect on their own circumstances which will result in shared empathy. Also remember the emotional journey — balance the emotions of your speech and be aware of the mountain or rollercoaster you're climbing. Use humour in the body if you need to release some tension.

> "Remember, your story is for your audience and your questions give them the opportunity to reflect on their own circumstances which will result in shared empathy."

You will have space for one or two short stories in your body, so look at your bare bones and detail the specifics of the story. Remember to use dialogue — think about the conversations that defined the episode: who said what to whom? If you were bullied, what did your bully say? If you got married, what were the words exchanged and how did you propose? On what night? What did it feel and look like? Use words to paint pictures and engage the five senses.

You may have to trim some details later to make the 7 minute mark, but the important thing right now is to get as much detail and information as possible out of your story to help determine what is important. *Consider these questions:*

- Are there important pieces of dialogue that I must say?

- What power questions will I ask?

- How will I transition from the body to the conclusion?

## Your conclusion

It is important to deliver your conclusion with passion while selling your message. If you have a foundational phrase, repeat it because repetition will help your message stay with your audience.

You may have reached the climactic scene towards the end of the body, or you may have the climax attached to your conclusion, but as your speech draws to a close, show your audience how you've changed, what you've learned, and leave them with your message.

*"I was 10 years old, my dad was in Nigeria, and whenever I asked my mum for pocket money she would say, "Do I look like a bank? I walk to work – how do you expect to get pocket money?"*

After years of being bullied and that incident with Terry, I was scarred emotionally. I would look in the mirror and think, "You are worthless." Every time I failed a school test, I would say, "You are worthless." If you could see a picture of how I felt, you would see a shipwreck – the pieces of wood represent the broken parts of my life. I felt like nothing. My bullies had stolen everything precious: my self-worth, my pride, and my confidence, and I woke up feeling empty, worried and worthless.

Have you ever been shipwrecked? Have the pirates ever plundered anything precious from you? What made matters worse for me was that I wanted comfort, but as a teenager, comfort means girlfriend! It was hard to find a girlfriend – the odds were stacked against me: first of all, I went to an all-boys school, and secondly, no money meant I couldn't afford even a cinema ticket and girls expected guys to pay – my wife still does; some things never change!"

Mildred was a God-send. She walked into my life and put my ship back together again. It wasn't her soft words or her sweet smile, it's because of the day she looked me in the eye and said, "You are worth it!" I thought I was worthless, but all along I was worth it. It just took a brown-skinned girl with sweet brown eyes to remind me. I started to look in the mirror and say, "I am worth it!" I started to take up sports again, and while I played, I would say, "I am worth it!" Then I put a ring on Mildred's finger and told her that she's worth it, too.

You can survive any shipwreck, you can climb any mountain, and you can turn your life around. You may need a Mildred to help you along, but even if you don't have a Mildred, everyone has a mirror. If you can stand facing that mirror and say, "I am worth it," then your self-worth will come swimming back to you. So the choice is yours: what will you say in the mirror . . . are you worth it?"

In my example conclusion here, I use power lines, word pictures, the rule of three, and you-focused questions to inspire my audience. The conclusion is also a good place to paint scenarios that are easily relatable to your audience, but remember, no matter how passionate you get, you need to practice your passion!

> "Remember, no matter how passionate you get in your conclusion, you need to practice your passion!"

Consider these questions for your conclusion:

- Will I use call backs?

- What scenarios will I paint?

- What power lines will I include?

- What will be my call to action?

At the end of your speech writing session, you would have transitioned from the bare bones, which were five or six lines, to approximately 30 lines of your almost-complete speech. The above example is 433 words, so to make a 7 minute speech, I would have to expand and add a few more details. I could do this in the introduction, body, or conclusion.

As what I've shared is a personal story, it was very easy for me to lay out the bare bones and finish writing it, but the bare bones method works with any type of story you want to tell. Using this technique, the example speech above took me less than an hour to write — when you read and understand the techniques and the 7 minute formula, you can get a draft version of your speech in no time at all!

# CHAPTER 9:

## THE FOUR T'S TO A TANTALISING TITLE

There are many ways to excite and impact your audience on the platform, but there are also techniques you must use off the platform to anticipate this effect, even before you open your mouth! If you've ever been to a big seminar or convention, you would have picked up an event programme with a list of speakers and their topic titles. Often, we have no other information about the speech or presentation, and we must decide whether to attend the session by the speech title alone.

It's no coincidence that the best speakers have great titles: Tony Robbins has "Unlimited Power" and "Awaken the Giant"; Les Brown has "Unlock Your Inner Greatness"; Brian Tracy has "Four Steps to Getting Past Obstacles". These accomplished speakers know that great speaking starts off the platform. You too can harness this technique by applying the four T's to a tantalising title. Follow these steps to connect with your audience before you even say a word.

### 'T' is for TRAILER . . .

If you've ever seen a film trailer, you'll know that it usually includes the best highlights from the film. Not too much to ruin the plot, but just enough for the audience to know what to expect. In much the same way, your speech title can either tantalise or terrify your audience!

> "The trick is to use a title that is not only exciting, but also captures the essence of what the audience can expect from your speech."

The trick is to use a title that is not only exciting, but also captures the essence of what the audience can expect from your speech. For example, "The 7 Secret Steps to Becoming an Entrepreneur" serves as a far better trailer than something vague and bland like "Entrepreneurialism". With the former title, audience members know exactly what to expect: aspiring entrepreneurs will sign up quickly, while seasoned business people will look elsewhere, all because of the enticing trailer.

## 'T' is for TEASE . . .

Sometimes it is good to tease your audience before you speak – seduce their ears, make them curious, and they will be excited to hear what you've got to say. Have you ever had someone come up to you and say, "You'll never guess what just happened to me!" I don't know about you, but I automatically think, "What happened? Tell me more!" I've been teased into the conversation!

You can achieve the same effect with your speech title by using words and phrases that evoke curiosity. For example: "Five Secret Success Strategies", "What the Millionaires Won't Tell You", and "From Mistakes to Millions".

If you were in a speech contest, you could use teaser titles like: "Snakebite" (by Craig Valentine), "Three Silver Bullets" (by David Brooks), or "Which Dog Are You Stroking?" (by Erick Raney). These titles all evoke curiosity and tease the audience into wanting to hear more.

The tease evokes curiosity and creates anticipation – but make sure you meet those expectations with your content and delivery!

## 'T' is for TICKLE . . .

A title that tickles simply makes the audience laugh. At the 2001 World Championship of Public Speaking, Darren LaCroix's took home the trophy with a speech called "Ouch!" The first time I heard the title it made me snigger, and when watching the video I could hear a few sniggers in the audience, too. Imagine the live introduction: "With a speech entitled 'Ouch!', please welcome Darren LaCroix!"

A title tickle is especially appropriate for a humorous speech because it immediately gets the audience laughing, which in turn relaxes them and makes them anticipate a good time ahead. Jim Key has a keynote speech titled "What to do when your frog won't sing". My friend, Douglas Dewar, had a speech titled,

"How to medicate your cat . . . the easy way", and another friend, Garreth Garrels, won the Humorous Speaking Championship in 2010 with a speech called, "I got beaten up by a girl".

> "A title tickle is especially appropriate for a humorous speech because it immediately gets the audience laughing, which in turn relaxes them and makes them anticipate a good time ahead."

This technique can also work for speeches that aren't strictly humorous in content. If you decide to use the tickle in your next title, make sure it is relevant to your speech content and I promise you, most of your audience will be ticklish!

## 'T' is for TWIST . . .

A title twist can work in two ways: The first is to create a speech title which has a twist from the norm and delivers something unexpected. For example: "How To Get Married . . . For the Fourth Time"; or "The Six Benefits of Not Going to University". Both of these titles initially imply a standard speech, but the twist comes in to lead the audience down a different path. A twist within the title implies that the speaker might be different and interesting and therefore worth listening to.

The second way to use the twist is to use a seemingly predictable title, but then follow it up with a very unpredictable speech. I can think of no better master at this technique than Wayne Malcolm, one of the UK's best public speakers and life coaches.

One of Wayne's speeches, "The Laws of Finishing", outlines four laws of finishing or completing a goal, including the laws of time management and self-discipline. Towards the climax of the speech, he reveals that the final law of finishing is the most important law and then he goes on to reveal this final law as faith — "Once you have faith, it is already finished!" This is a big twist because the audience were led to believe that they would be receiving tips on the hard work they must do to finish and achieve their goals; but in the end, it turned out that the final and most important law is to nothing to do with hard work at all — just simply believe and have faith.

In this second twist method, the title will imply that the speech is going in a certain direction, but midway through your delivery, there will be an unexpected twist which surprises the audience and reveals that the title was actually a metaphor all along!

Another example from Wayne is a speech called "The Coming Wealth Transfer", a speech about the transfer of wealth from the rich to the poor. When he delivers this speech, audience members tend to assume that he is speaking about money; however, halfway through the speech he reveals, "Many people think that the wealth transfer is a transfer of money, but the coming wealth transfer is really a transfer of knowledge" and then goes on to describe the value of knowledge as the only true wealth.

> "The twist technique will only work well if the title initially seems predictable – the trick is to use a common title and give an unusual speech."

This twist technique will only work well if the title initially seems predictable – the trick is to use a common title and give an unusual speech.

Next time you have a speech to write, apply one of these techniques to your title and you will be tantalising your audience in no time!

# CHAPTER 10:

# DELIVERING YOUR 7 MINUTE MASTERPIECE

Writing a winning speech is one thing but delivering a winning speech is another! The way you use the stage, combined with your words and message, can make or break your speech. If you don't know how to use the stage, you may miss an opportunity to effectively deliver your message, or worse still, you may be a distraction to your audience.

My wife was at a seminar once and half an hour into the seminar, she sent me a text message which said, "Darling, the speakers in this seminar are all pacers. It's so distracting!" When she got home, she told me that the speakers were walking from one side of the stage to the other, back and forth, all through their speeches. After five minutes of their pacing, she wanted to yell at them, "Why on earth are you moving so much?" They were moving because they didn't know what else to do and it was distracting because their movements didn't support their words.

Moving should always appear natural and fluid, not rigid. Before adding a move to your delivery, always ask yourself, "Is my movement matching and illustrating my story or my message?" Always record and review your practice session so that you can evaluate whether your movements are natural and not distracting.

> "Moving should always appear natural and fluid, not rigid. Before adding a move to your delivery, always ask yourself, 'Is my movement matching and illustrating my story or my message?'"

Remember to check new stages before you speak, because every platform is different, and the one you're on today may not be the same as the one you were on yesterday. Base your delivery tools on what space you have available to you.

If you don't know how to use the stage effectively, you risk losing your audience's attention. Below are a few delivery tools to get you started on the right path, and if you need more help with your staging, coaching is a good way to get useful feedback and advice.

# Holograms

In popular terminology, a hologram is a projected three-dimensional representation of a person or object, normally used in communication, entertainment or security features (like on your credit card). Holograms are quite popular in science fiction movies, but when you deliver a speech, you can create your own "holograms". I first heard of public speaking holograms from Darren LaCroix (although speakers have always used this technique, he coined the phrase in a public speaking context).

A hologram in stage delivery is the planting of an imaginary object, place or character on the stage with the use of body language and gestures. If used correctly, holograms can take your delivery to a whole new level.

## Plant an object

In one of my speeches, "Slap Back", I have a line that says: "I lifted up the doormat and picked up the key . . ." As I say this, I physically act out bending down and lifting up an invisible doormat at a certain place on the stage. A few lines later, I say,"so I went back to the doormat and put the key back." I return to the same spot and lift up the imaginary doormat. This helps the audience visualise my story and it makes the delivery more interesting to watch.

The rule here is to only plant the most significant object, or your speech will become confusing and distracting. I have planted objects such as doors, chairs, rollercoasters, doormats, and roundabouts and I have found it to be a powerful delivery tool.

## Plant a place

I often hear speakers say, "So I went to my mother's house," or "I went on holiday," and as they say these words they are standing still. This is okay, but an okay delivery is not a winning delivery! When you speak about places, locations or travelling, consider planting that spot on the stage and interact physically with it.

> "When you speak about places, locations or travelling, consider planting that spot on the stage and interact physically with it."

In Keep on Walking, I repeated the phrase, "I was back in the tunnel again" three times. When I watched a recording of my delivery, I realised I had three tunnels in three different places! What a mess! It was still an okay delivery, but it must have been very confusing for my audience.

When I worked further on my delivery, I knew I had to plant one specific place for the tunnel – a designated place on the stage that I could point to or walk towards when I said the words. Planting this place dramatically improved the conclusion of my speech. By the conclusion, all I needed to do was point to the "tunnel" I had created: "When life throws it worst at you, you have two choices: to stay trapped in a tunnel (*point to my planted place*) or to keep on walking."

## Plant a character

You can also plant a character by describing the character, moving slightly to the left or right, or imitating their posture or voice when you deliver their dialogue. This helps your audience follow your script and characters better, and it also helps them visualise the character. You might not need to do this with every character; it's usually more effective if you just plant the most significant character.

## Use a prop

Props are a powerful delivery tool that can support your words and message. J.A. Gamache, a multiple world finalist, used a chair in one of his speeches to illustrate his "grand papa". Every time he had a conversation with his grand papa, he would walk to the chair and "converse" with it. In his very personal story, his grand papa dies and to represent his mood and loss, J.A. places the chair on the ground. It was a powerful use of a prop, and it greatly enhanced the flow and imagery of the speech. I can still feel the impact that speech had on me today.

## Create a timeline

Most speakers use their hands to describe timelines, such as Monday, Tuesday, Wednesday and so on. I have found that creating a timeline can be useful to guide your audience through the passing of time in your speech. Start with the earliest date in your story, and for every date or time period, move along the stage. For example, I could say:

> "In my first years as a football player (move slightly left), I was okay. In my second year as a footballer (move further to the left), I was good. In my third year as a footballer (move to the farthest left), I was great."

> "Creating a timeline can be useful to guide your audience through the passing of time in your speech."

Now I have created a timeline that my audience can physically follow. I can now go back to the "first year" space on the stage and tell a short story.

## Split the stage

Splitting the stage is simply "dividing" your stage into two or three parts to help illustrate your points. For example, if you were talking about the difference between men and women, you could divide the stage into two parts: on one side, you would speak about women, and on the other side you would speak about men.

I remember being impressed the first time I saw Jonah Mungoshi, a 2002 third place world finalist, deliver a speech which included stories about Mother Teresa, Ghandi, and Nelson Mandela. He split the stage into three components and told three different stories from each person's life. His meaning and intentions were so clear and this is turn made his message clear and poignant to the audience. He placed third in the world.

## Plant yourself

When I speak of "planting yourself", I am not speaking of using a hologram but of staying planted right in the middle of the stage and not moving at all.

The two places in your speech where you want to stay planted are the beginning and the conclusion. These start and end times are the best opportunities to both connect with your audience (by using eye contact) and sell your message by taking all the action out and showing your sincerity. Be earnest and gimmick-free as you drive home your message and call your audience to action.

## Practice, practice, practice!

The only way to be natural and spontaneous on stage is to practice, practice, practice! The best advice I've ever heard is that you need to know your speech so well that you can become spontaneous on stage. Memorise or internalise your words and delivery – the last thing you want is to be mentally searching for words during your 7 minutes.

Memorising both your introduction and conclusion is a good way to make sure you have a strong beginning and ending, and it leaves you room to improvise and be spontaneous with stories in the body. Another option is to memorise the whole script or you could opt to only memorise important lines and phrases and internalise the outline. Feel free to use whichever method works best for you.

> "Memorising both your introduction and conclusion is a good way to make sure you have a strong beginning and ending."

Where should you practice? Everywhere – in your car, bed, living room, even in the bathroom! It's also good to practice on the event stage or a similar platform, where possible, to become more comfortable, and of course, practicing in front of a video camera is invaluable.

One important thing to remember is that your audience members do not know if you forget your words so even if this happens on stage after you've practiced, don't broadcast it, keep on going!

# CHAPTER 11:

## EVALUATING YOUR MASTERPIECE

Is there a way to transform a good speech into a great one? Yes, there is, but it will take humility and discernment. The best way to take your good speech to the great level is to seek evaluation before your final presentation.

### What is an evaluation?

An evaluation is any feedback you receive on your speech and delivery. An evaluation can be from other people or from yourself if you're reviewing your own recordings.

I only received one evaluation before the district finals. I used to boast about this until I realised that if I had more feedback, especially from experts and champions, I could have strengthened my speech dramatically. The one evaluation I did receive, however, helped me refine my speech, and I wouldn't have reached the finals without it.

> "I only received one evaluation before the district finals. I used to boast about this until I realised that if I had more feedback, especially from experts and champions, I could have strengthened my speech dramatically."

Before the semi-final rounds, I visited an advanced Toastmasters club full of experienced speakers who had all completed their beginner manuals and were working on advanced modules. I was there to practice Keep on Walking so I asked the very experienced audience to give me feedback on my speech and delivery. Their feedback – some verbal, some written – was invaluable and helped form my two personal laws of evaluation:

### 1) Take what resonates

I have had evaluations from some of the most seasoned speakers and coaches where I have understood their point but it didn't necessarily resonate with me. On these occasions, I had to stick to my guns and go with my gut feelings because only I am responsible for what I take to the stage.

### 2) Out of the mouth of two or three, make an adjustment

If I receive a set of evaluations and they all say the same thing, such as "Add more pauses", "Smile more", "Build better characters" . . . then I take it on board, as humbling as it may be.

There are different dimensions of evaluations that I used on my journey and still use today which can work for you too:

## Self-evaluation

You can evaluate yourself, your speech and your delivery in several ways but the best way is to buy a video camera and an audio recorder. By taping your delivery, you can evaluate your speech without needing an audience. I do this quite often, especially early in the writing and practicing stages of building a speech. I watch my facial expression, gestures, and stage positions, and I listen for my pace and tone. I check for the general feel of my presentation and delivery. Am I excited by it? What do I like? What do I want to cut? What do I need to add? Self-evaluating this way helps inspire ideas and reaffirms what should be kept or deleted.

You can also self-evaluate by being very aware of your audience and their responses while delivering your speech. Note the good and the bad and then adapt your presentation where necessary.

> "By taping your delivery, you can evaluate your speech without needing an audience."

The only way that self-evaluations can work in your favour is if you are aware of potential pitfalls. You must understand the science of speaking and know tools and tricks for improvement, otherwise you may delete what is good and keep what is bad!

## Response to conversations

I usually test the stories and metaphors that I will use in my speech in everyday conversation. I tell the bare bones of a story to a friend or colleague in two to three minutes (it's hard to find a captive audience for a 7 minute speech unless they are a speech coach or at a Toastmasters Club). If the person with whom I'm conversing seems bored or does not respond well, I drop or tweak the idea and try again with someone else.

Experience makes this a more valuable method of self-evaluation – I have done this so many times that I now have a sense for what will or won't work. Sometimes I catch myself telling a good story, and I write it down as soon as possible to see if I can build on it.

## Speech coaching

Coaching has been the best form of evaluation that I have received. After winning the UK and Ireland Speech Contest, I asked Jim Key to be my coach. I sent him videos of my delivery and a copy of my script and his feedback taught me a lot of the knowledge that I have gained in my speaking career.

Coaches shorten your learning curve. A coach has an eye for things that you may have missed and a good coach will not only tell you what to do, they will teach you *why* you need to make certain adjustments. Every world class speaker has had many evaluations before they hit the stage – even elite speakers still have coaches and can testify that coaching helped them earn their crowns.

When you are being coached, remember that your coach is just a human being and not everything he or she says is gospel – you still have the choice. It is also important that your coach is an expert in their field, otherwise it is just another opinion. A good way to determine whether an evaluator is a good coach is to ask them to explain their reasoning for suggested changes. If they can clearly explain their reasoning and it resonates with you, take the advice, knowing you are in safe hands.

> **"When you are being coached, remember that your coach is just a human being and not everything he or she says is gospel – you still have the choice."**

## Group evaluations

Group evaluations give you a chance to get more eyes and ears on your speech. Group evaluations involve an audience gathering together to listen to and evaluate your speech.

This happens frequently at Toastmasters clubs. The audience members are given evaluation forms and asked to give feedback on the speeches they hear. This type of evaluation is extremely helpful because you get a variety of responses to the very same material and delivery. Group evaluations provide insight on how different audience members think and feel during your speech.

I received a group evaluation two rounds before the UK and Ireland contest and in this, I received a variety of responses from, "That was fantastic" to, "You need to pause". Even though I found both comments helpful, I know that hearing that I was fantastic wouldn't improve my speech, it just made me feel good about myself! I needed more constructive feedback to help me build a better speech so I have learned to embrace the evaluations that will hurt my ego along with the ones that build it up. Always keep in mind though that group evaluations are just opinions – only you have the final say on your speech.

Evaluations make you excel – they are a crucial component to your 7 minute masterpiece so always aim to get as many evaluations as possible before your speaking engagement. If you're in a contest, try to get a coach to help, but at a minimum, engage in some self-evaluation and you'll be one step closer to 7 minute greatness.

> "Evaluations make you excel – they are a crucial component to your 7 minute masterpiece so always aim to get as many evaluations as possible before your speaking engagement."

# CHAPTER 12:

## IN HINDSIGHT (MY 7 MINUTE PERSPECTIVE)

Entering the Toastmasters International Speech Contest was the experience of a lifetime for me. Not only was I fortunate enough to win all regional contest levels, I had the bonus of travelling to Las Vegas, competing internationally, and making new friends.

I'll be honest; at times the process was painful – imagine editing and re-writing for what feels like the hundredth time, feeling like a prisoner practicing in a room all by yourself, always asking if there is just one more word you can tweak, cut or add, and then trying to sit still and wait for the judges' decision at the contest with your family and friends beside you, and you wondering if you've done enough to win or even place?!

Despite all these emotions and the stress of the whole process, it was all worth it. Lives were touched and transformed during my 7 minutes. Along the way, I discovered a gift that I didn't know I had and through hard work and practice, turned it into a skill.

For much of my journey, I wasn't aware of any of the techniques I eventually employed. Even when I wrote the first, rough draft of Keep on Walking, before I had any coaching and input, I felt it was pretty good. It's possible that I already had a sense of what makes a good speech because I had been exposed to good

> "You may discover as you grow as a speaker that what you once did instinctually, after training, coaching and evaluation, you eventually do intentionally."

speaking while growing up, including listening to preachers and watching movies.

After receiving coaching, reading books and studying other resources, I discovered that there were techniques I had applied unconsciously. You may discover the same thing as you grow as a speaker – what you once did instinctually, after training, coaching and evaluation, you eventually do intentionally. Knowledgeable coaches will help you transform from talented to skilful.

## Coaches, family and friends

My wife, Jim Key, Dave Sellman, and Phillip Khan-Panni were my coaches for the final version of the speech I delivered in Las Vegas. There were lots of changes in the delivery aspect of the speech as I practiced before the contest.

One of the suggestions that I employed was the use of a hologram, an empty spot on the stage that represents my tunnel. I also use my jacket and bags not only as props, but also as a metaphor to show how I repaired the broken pieces of my life during the climax of my speech. I worked on my facial expressions, such as making sure I was smiling during the inspiring section of my speech and expressing frustration at the sadder moments. Jim told me that when he saw me win the UK and Ireland Speech Contest, my passion was written all over my face. He said I looked angry, and after I reviewed the recording of the contest, I realised he was right so I made sure I smiled in Las Vegas – I smiled a *whole* lot!

The journey to a successful 7 minute speech may be a long, sometimes painful, road, but here are some benefits I experience along the way which you may find in your own journey too:

- I gained the knowledge that my speech helped people in dark situations;

- I made new friends at the events I attended and/or spoke at;

- I discovered my talent and developed skills;

- I was coached by World Champion speakers;

- I learned priceless principles about public speaking;

- I won a trip to Las Vegas;

- I received a trophy;

- I was inducted into the District 71 Hall of Fame;

- I now get booked for paid speaking engagements.

You may never enter a speech contest but if you prepare like you are competing, when you hit the stage you will win every time, and after all your hard work, you will definitely be rewarded for igniting, impacting and inspiring your audience.

## What would I change about Keep on Walking?

I know that Keep on Walking is a good speech, but I also know it's not a perfect speech (because there is no such thing!). The speech grew with me, and as I have grown and expanded my skills since the last time I presented it, I have reflected on changes I would make if I were to present it again:

### 1) I would be more conversational

When I first thought about delivering Keep on Walking outside of a Toastmasters setting, I had a mind block. It was written for a speech contest which means I planted words in the script that I wouldn't necessarily use in everyday conversation.

Keep on Walking is packed with alliteration, metaphors, similes, word pictures and other tools of the trade, including a strong foundational phrase. The only problem is that some of the lines are so smooth, it is easy to tell that certain parts of the speech were written, planned and constructed. This is fine for a Toastmasters contest where your use of words is put to the test, but outside of a contest, you want your audience to feel engaged in a personal conversation with you.

Does this mean that I would not write my speech out now? No it doesn't — to quote Darren LaCroix once more, "The best speeches are not written, they are re-written." It is upon this principle that I now build my best speeches. It is definitely possible to be well prepared and still sound conversational.

To achieve a more conversational feel, I would have toned down the alliteration and repetition. I would add words and phrases that I use every day, and maybe add a few more questions. In my presentations outside Toastmasters, I still use alliteration, repetition, and rhyme, but not to such a degree that it sounds forced.

### 2) *I may lose some of the props*

As I have grown and matured in my public speaking career, I have come to realise than any small thing can distract an audience. I would consider whether my use of props enhance or detract from the overall presentation. This decision might also change depending on the age group and type of the audience I'm speaking to. For instance, if I am speaking to a group of young adults, I would use several props to engage them. If I were talking to a group of mature adults, the props may serve as a distraction, so I may select only one or two props to use.

### 3) *I would answer this question: "What kept you walking?"*

While I feel Keep on Walking had a clear message enhanced by a moving emotional journey, describing the motivation of *why* I wanted to and did keep on walking would have fully enriched my audience members' experience. If I shared what it was that kept me walking, this would have enhanced the effectiveness of my speech.

### 4) *I would consider coaching – more of it and earlier on in the process*

The benefits of coaching and the power of evaluations became clear to me as I moved up the levels of contest speaking. Had I known what I know now, I would have engaged coaches and sought more peer evaluations before the contest started and during the earlier rounds.

I only had one formal evaluation before the finals of the UK and Ireland Speech Contest – imagine if I had more!

## In closing . . .

So there you have it – we have gone behind the veil of a champion speech preparation and delivery, and you now have the tools and techniques to impact, ignite and inspire every audience you address.

It's time to win on every level – both the honours and the hearts. I hope you will find *7 Minutes to Win It* a useful resource every time you are called upon to deliver a speech or presentation.

Please stay in touch — I would love to know how your speaking improves as you apply the principles you have learned. If you have any questions, need any support or want to share your 7 minute masterpiece with me, you can email me at hello@malachitalabi.com.

Never forget that your audience deserves your best, and here's to our new mantra:

**"Give me 7 seconds and I'll tell you a joke; give me 7 minutes and I will touch your life . . ."**

# BONUS CHAPTER:

## WHAT HAPPENED IN VEGAS

In Las Vegas in August 2011, myself and eight other contestants stood and waited for the result of our semi-final speech contest. The judge said: "The third place winner is . . . Malachi Talabi. The second place winner is . . . Garret Garrels (who I had the opportunity to interview about his experience for my Conversations with Champions audio – for a 15-minute snippet go to http://champions.malachitalabi.com) . . .")

When the judge came round to announcing the first place winner, there was no suspense, we knew who it would be – Scott Pritchard. I had the privilege of watching Scott deliver his excellent speech in Vegas and in this bonus chapter, he shares the story behind his glory.

### Scott Pritchard's story

In 2011 I was the third place winner in the World Championship of Public Speaking. The contest took place over six months featuring over 25,000 contestants.

People from my past had always suggested that I get into life coaching and professional speaking. These comments usually went in one ear and out the other. At the age of 45 I finally went to my first Toastmasters meeting. I married myself to learning the skills of a professional speaker. I spoke five to seven times a week at Kiwanis, Rotary clubs, Chamber of Commerce meetings and at church. I would record every speech and critique it at length.

Two years later, I was the third place winner in the World Championship. Where in your life are you putting something off that you have often thought about trying?

I was at a Darren LaCroix event in December 2009 when he said, "Speakers who are funny, make more money." I thought to myself, "The more money I make, the more people I can help!" That evening, I went to my first open mic night at Bonkerz Comedy Club at Palace Station Casino in Las Vegas, Nevada. I did not get one laugh. I went with a friend who had stand up comedy experience, but like myself, he did not get a single laugh either. The difference between he and I is that I kept coming back. Eventually I started getting laughs. I kept what worked and threw out everything else. I committed myself to professional speaking and stand-up comedy.

One night in May 2010 I was performing at an open mic at Grind Burger located across from the University of Nevada, Las Vegas campus. It just so happened that two bookers from LA Comedy Club, Matt and Joaquin, were on hand and heard my set. They liked my stage presence, confidence and that my content was clean. They invited me to do a guest spot on an off night at the Four Queens Hotel Casino in Downtown Las Vegas in a paid comedy club. It went well, to the point that I started doing guest spots on weekends and eventually hosting.

Since November 2010 I have been hosting and doing stand-up comedy at LA Comedy Club at Planet Hollywood on the strip. This afforded me the opportunity to hob-knob and hang out with other comics who are already travelling the world, living the comedic dream. Because of this experience I am now a paid stand-up comedian who got my jumpstart by opening for Louis Anderson in the midwest and later a famous country singer, Lorrie Morgan.

It's never too late to accomplish anything. It is a matter of getting your mind right, which has to do with tunnel vision. I have read that if you want to change your life, change your mind. It is true. It worked for me. If it worked for me, it will work for you. What is it in your life that you have yet to accomplish that is near and dear to your heart? I went from zero to doing stand-up comedy and hosting on the strip in Las Vegas within twelve months. I'd like to remind you that it is never too late. By getting in the game and making a decision to pursue public speaking and stand-up comedy, I am now performing all over the United States and look forward to performing internationally.

It's never too late to touch someone even after you're gone. Cheryl Kremer has been gone since May 18th 1980, yet she continues to touch lives. She touched me and by sharing her story to the world, I am, through Cheryl, touching many, many people. Every year in April, I speak and donate money to one senior at Valley High School in Elgin, Iowa, the school she graduated from. I select one senior who best represents the spirit of Cheryl Kremer. She will continue to touch lives long after I am gone because of her message, 'A touch can do so much.'

# PART 4:
## WINNING SPEECHES & USEFUL RESOURCES

This section of the book contains winning speeches from champions Scott Pritchard, Lisa Panarello, Omar Rivas, Granard McClendon, Dhanashree Thangaraja, Arnita Jones and Phil Barth, as well as useful resources for your speaking growth.

All the speeches in this section are also featured in the *7 Minute Champions* audio. What's interesting is that if you listen to the audio, you are likely to hear differences — some subtle, some more marked — between the written speech and the live performances. Sometimes the speech you write is not exactly the speech you deliver.

# The Laws of the Playground

## Winning speech by Malachi Talabi

### 2010 Area 35 (south East England) Humorous Speech Champion

"Guess what?"
"Snot."
"Guess why?"
"Bogie pie."

Welcome to the playground where children's songs are nursery rhymes and they get to the top of the charts; where Vladimir is the big bad bully and skipping ropes turn into whipping ropes.

I recently got a job as a TA which is short for Teaching Assistant, although it should be short for Terrorist Attendant – you should be able to tell by my hair.

Ghastly Gillian, Mrs Monster McCluckin took me on a tour of the borough's worst school. It was a chamber of challenging children – we had them all: crooks and criminals, thugs and thieves, rouges and rascals. I needed the money though and I, Mr Talabi, was called in to calm the crisis.

I was thrust into the playground like a bat out of hell. All the kids came running towards me: "Hello sir, hello sir . . ."

One of them caught my eye. You couldn't miss him – his name was "Pick Nose Paul", it was written all over his chest. I watched as his finger went on a voyage through his nose. He discovered an iceberg, seconds later this gigantic iceberg of a bogie was swimming in his saliva. Paul decided he wanted to have a bogie snack instead of a kit-kat. "Hello . . ." He wanted to shake my hand.

What would you do? What was I going to do?

"Play time's over!"

Playground principle number one: first impressions count.

Have you got any bad habits in your life that stop people from connecting with you . . . ? Clean them up.

Tuesday was the second day on playground duty and it was a shocker. "Charlie, Charlie, Charlie . . ." "Sir, Charlie's winning a race!" Chubby Charlie NEVER ran – trying to get Charlie to run was like trying to teach a tortoise how to tango.

But today was different. Vladimir had brought a chilli cheese burger into the playground. Charlie sniffed, whiffed, and soared towards the cheese burger. Chubby Charlie's chasing a chilly cheeseburger. Chubby Charlie's chasing a chilli cheese burger! He's running faster than a train – is it a bird? Is it a plane? No, it's Chubby Charlie chasing a chilli cheese burger!

What would you do? I couldn't let it happen.

"Play time's over!"

Playground principle number two: desire your destiny

What will it take for you to run in life? A chilli cheese burger?

I loved my job – this wasn't work, I was learning principles for life!

So on Thursday I ran in but all hell broke loose – "Fight, fight, fight . . ." In the red corner Vladimir the Vicious. Vladimir was tall as a tree with football-sized fists. In the other corner nerdy Nigel. Nigel had one tooth imprisoned by metal braces – he had no chance.

I'm on duty and I'm scared! I didn't want a black eye blacker than a black hole, a bleeding nose redder than the red sea, a headache worse than a hurricane!

Vladimir throws a punch; Nigel rolls through his legs. Vladimir falls face first into the mud pit. "Nigel, Nigel, Nigel!"

"Play time's over!"

Playground principle number three: wisdom is better than strength – don't work harder, work smarter.

It's Friday now and I can't wait to get to work. I've had ringside tickets to the fight of the century and I've watched Chubby Charlie chase a chilli cheese burger. I get to the playground and today there's just one note: "Ip, dip, do – the joke's on you; we are playing hide and seek to be found by you!"

"Play time's over!"

Playground principle number four: expect the unexpected.

Toastmasters and guests, life is a playground. You need to know that if you are going to run in life, then you need to desire your destiny, wisdom is better than strength, and remember to expect the unexpected.

# 1980: A Touch Can Do So Much
## Winning Speech by Scott Pritchard

### 2011 World Champion of Public Speaking 3rd Place Winner

Where were you the first time you met someone who touched you emotionally? A touch can do so much.

Most people in Las Vegas are from somewhere else. I was born in a 3rd world country in Central America, Iowa. Fact is I love Iowa, it's where I was raised. Come back with me to 1980, I'm 15, a sophomore in high school. As I'm walking down a crowded school hallway, upperclassman and wise guy Dan Lott knocks my books out of my hand.

As I'm scrambling trying to retrieve my homework and all I see are knees and feet when on my elbow I feel a touch, "Here, let me help you." Her name is Cheryl Kremer, the prettiest girl I've ever seen. She looks at me and says, "Hey I know you, you're Randy's brother." For the first time in my life I was a somebody. I look up to Randy because he's taller and now he's dating the prettiest girl in school, Cheryl.

One week later after basketball practice, Randy says, "Scott we're going to stop by and see Cheryl, it's on the way home." We diverted 13 miles. At Cheryl's house, I see the ugliest, meanest dog who would not stop growling at us. Cheryl's sister says, "It's ok guys, Buster hates everyone. You see, he was run over by a tractor, he has a bad leg and a broken tail, he growls at everyone except Cheryl."

Just then she appears, pretty and petite and this mean ferocious dog turns into a pussycat, as he awkwardly and hurriedly runs to Cheryl on three legs. She picks him up and starts to pet him lovingly. I swear I can hear him purring as he's wagging that broken tail.

Cheryl says, "Buster understands, a touch can do so much." On the way home I ask Randy, "Why Cheryl?"

He replies "She's beautiful, but it's more than that. She's a good person; she wants to become a nurse, she cares." During the next few weeks it becomes obvious to me why everyone loves Cheryl, it's because she loves everyone. As pretty as she is, she's ten times prettier on the inside.

Do you remember your high school graduation day? For Randy and Cheryl it's Sunday May 18th, 1980 a beautiful day. After the graduation, I see Cheryl smiling from ear to ear wearing a pink dress and holding a red rose.

I eagerly approach her, "Congratulations, I'll see you at our party tonight! Are you a little sad that this is the end?"

She takes my hand, in her eyes I see a spark, "Scott, this is not the end, this is the beginning. I want to be a nurse so I can help those who can't help themselves. A touch can do so much. I'll see you tonight."

A few hours later my friends and I leave Randy's graduation party in Mike's pickup. A half mile from our farmhouse on a narrow gravel road as we're approaching a hill we're involved in a head on collision.

As I wake up in the middle of the road, I see a car crushed into Mike's pickup. I yell, "Mike, check the passengers, I'll help the driver." A few moments later Mike says, "These girls are in bad shape but they're alive. Scott, how's the driver?"

With tears filling my eyes, I respond, "She's dead. It's Cheryl."

Three days later at the funeral Cheryl was buried wearing a pink dress and cradling a red rose after the funeral. I'm sitting in Randy's car thinking about the last conversation I had with her. She was so up, positive and excited about touching lives. I will always remember the way she touched me that day.

As Randy starts to drive away a song comes on the radio. It was Bette Midler's, 'The Rose'. Randy is upset and I ask, "Are you okay?" "No, no, no! I'm not okay, this was Cheryl's favourite song."

Cheryl has been gone since 1980 yet she continues to touch lives. She has had a profound effect on my life. I see her whenever I see kindness, innocence and compassion. She touched Randy's life: he was reckless and a rebel. She had a calming effect on him forever. In 1983 he married a gal and they've been together ever since.

If dogs could talk, what do you think Buster would say?

In your life emotionally, physically or spiritually are you touching someone? Why not everyone? It could be helping someone, spending time with a young person or offering a word of encouragement.

When I first met Cheryl in that crowded school hallway in 1980 she touched my elbow and I realised, I'm not alone. Graduation day she touched my hand and I learned we all need a touch. Today she continues to touch my heart. A touch can do so much. 31 years after you're gone, will someone still feel your touch?

---

### BIOGRAPHY: SCOTT PRITCHARD

Scott Pritchard is an award-winning professional speaker and humorist. In 2011, during the World Championship of Public Speaking, Scott took 3rd place in the world – among 270,000 Toastmasters, he was the only American to place, making him America's top speaker.

In addition to speaking to audiences across the world, Scott resides in Las Vegas, where he does standup comedy on the Strip at Planet Hollywood every weekend, with his own show "Laugh and Stay Motivated". Scott is also an entrepreneur who operates many businesses in Las Vegas. He is living proof it is never too late to achieve your dreams by simply taking action.

For more information and to contact Scott, visit www.ScottPritchardSpeaks.com.

***Listen to *1980: A Touch Can Do So Much* in the 7 Minute Champions audio***

# What's "L" Got to Do With It?

## Winning speech by Lisa Panarello

### 2010 World Champion of Public Speaking Finalist

Mr. Contest Chair, fellow Toastmasters and guests, I find it truly amazing that with all the billions of people on this planet, there are still many times when one can feel lonely.

I'm sometimes lonely when I'm on a date. This one date, I got my hair done, put on this little black dress. I looked gooood. He picks me up and says "Uh, I'm wearing jeans 'cause it's Friday night." I thought, what do you wear on a Monday night, pajamas?

On another blind date, he arrives 45 minutes late. He calls and says, "Hi, I'm downstairs (click)." What, are your fingers broken? Ring the bell. I go downstairs, open the door. Not only did he not ring the bell, he stayed in the car, with his black tinted windows rolled up. I was scared. But I was hungry, so I went on the date.

I could go on all night with these stories, but I took a hard look at myself and realised of all the reasons I'm the reason that I'm still single. We don't have time to discuss all my faults.

But even when you're with someone you can feel lonely.

From ages 18 to 25 my arthritis was so bad I could barely walk or move my shoulder. I eventually had my wrist fused. We experience pain alone.

In 2004, I lost my mom to cancer, my best friend. 1,400 miles away we used to talk every day, and then she was gone. We suffer that kind of loss alone.

In 2008, we lost my younger brother to suicide. I was completely separated from the world that day. I used to throw up thinking about the day we got the call from the police. I used to cry violently. Sometimes I still do. No matter who's holding us, we cry inside alone.

Now, I'm pretty sure that everyone in this room has had some sort of tragedy or challenge they had to face alone. So what does "L" have to do with it? "L" is what I use to save myself from chronic loneliness. It's how I fill the void.

"L" is the LOVE I have for me and all that I am."L" is the LAUGHTER (pick up the paper scroll) for everything I'm not. "L" is the LUST I have for LIFE—everything in between.

We don't have time to 'wait' for someone else to make us happy. I've been single for over 20 years. Once my twin brother asked me, "How do you do it? My wife and kids are gone for two days and I'm going stir crazy." I said, 'I'm good company". I didn't mean it with conceit. It's just that I fill my time up with L.

For instance, love for my career. Careers don't define us, but considering we spend over 10 hours a day on the job, our careers make up over 1/3 of our lives. Shouldn't we at least like it?

Outside of work, I fill up my time with all the other things I love. Movies, museums, bowling, books, sports, music . . . I could be in a fowl mood. When a good song comes on the radio I snap back into a 'life's not so bad' reality and start jamming. I like being in my head.

While I'm at work and play, I laugh at myself. I laugh at my serious side, my silly side. There's a lot to laugh at. And when I'm done making fun of myself, I make fun of other people. Don't act like you don't do it. People-watching is fun stuff.

And do you know when I am least alone, when I'm with food. Isn't it all about the food? I have been to just about every family function, holiday, wedding, etc. alooone. What can you do? Sit in the corner and sulk? Nah, I EAT! Chicken Parmesan, Shrimp Cantonese, Sushi. I work out 5 days a week so I can eat.

And if you really want to fill a void, spend time with kids. There's nothing quite like the unconditional love from a child.

Two years ago, my nephew wrote me this birthday card:

*"In every heart is the people a person loves. But, now we're talking about a different kind of person. Aunt Lisa. She is so fun that she is like a magician. Every time someone would be bored, she would just tap her feet and the fun would begin.*

*Aunt Lisa has been around for 40 years now and that means she has been helping, supporting, loving and changing people's lives in a positive way for 40 years."*

Is that better than Hallmark, or what? He was 9, and he got me.

And I'm happy to say that someone else got me; last year I met the man of my dreams. And at 42, I can honestly say he was worth the wait—and the work. Without the work, where would the 'yeah!' or 'ahhh' moments be? Everything we want in life is worth the effort.

But while you search for that special someone or as you go through a challenging time feeling alone, don't give up, fill up—with a LOVE for who you are, LAUGHTER for everything around you and a LUST for all that life has to offer. Because to save yourself from chronic loneliness, "L" has got EVERYTHING to do with it!

---

## BIOGRAPHY: LISA PANARELLO

Lisa Panarello is an empowering career coach and the Founder & President of Careers Advance. Since 2001, Lisa has developed a revolutionary career-readiness curriculum, co-authored Unleash the Leader Within You!, produced The Power of A Smile DVD, and created over 2,000 groundbreaking resumes while helping thousands of individuals turn frustrating job search campaigns into exciting career journeys.

Simultaneously, Lisa has hit the stage with workshops, seminars and keynotes that have educated and inspired over 550,000 students, parents and professionals nationwide. In 2010, she rose above 30,000 international contestants to become a finalist in the Toastmasters International World Champion of Public Speaking Contest.

Today, Lisa drives the success of all those who seek to bridge a dream to reality. For more information and to contact Lisa, visit www.careersadvance.org.

***Listen to *What's "L" Got to Do With It?* in the 7 Minute Champions audio***

# The Box

## Winning speech by Omar Rivas

### 2011 World Champion of Public Speaking Finalist

"Toma . . . for you!"

"Thanks Mom! What is it?"

"It's a surprise!"

My mother had just given me an old, brown, hat box with worn edges, and a distinct "stuck in a closet for 14 years" smell. I didn't care as much about the box as what was IN the box. I started to peek inside the box, and she said "NO! Later." So out of respect . . . I put her gift away *(place the box on upper shelf in closet).*

Over the next two weeks, I asked her three separate times, "Mima . . . may I open your gift now?" Each time answering – "No! Later."

That box was looking more like a piñata right about now. Finally against everything I knew to be good and honorable – I took her gift out of the closet *(take box out of closet)* and opened it. *(Excited at first then confused)(Put the box on a pretend stool)*

Mr Contest Chair, Fellow Toastmasters, and everyone that has ever received an unexpected gift. That was 10 years ago, I was forty years old and I still felt horrible that I had gone against my mother's wishes. But it wasn't my birthday . . . . or Christmas, and I knew her failing memory would not allow her to remember the things that I liked, since her battle with Alzheimer's was becoming a losing war. But the box had nothing I ever expected.

A day or so later I approached her. *(pick up box from stool)* "Mima, I opened your gift. *(Act sorry)* I'm sorry. I know you asked me to wait – but – why did you give me this?"

She took the box *(she takes box from me),* looked inside, and a familiar confused look came over her face as if she had forgotten something important – again. She held the box close, and said – "It's my heart", in her Cuban accent. "Your heart?"

(*Gently*) "But Mima, there is nothing in the box, it's empty!!!" "NO!!!" (*Emphatic and defensive*) ". . . this box is not empty, it is filled with the many times you have touched my heart. It is filled with your love."

Once again she was making no sense at all. I was confused and frustrated. Do I go along with her delusion? Or do I correct her and let her know she placed nothing in the box?

Then, in what appeared to be a rare but lucid moment she looked at me and said (*in a broken Cuban accent*), "My son (*place box back on stool*) – you are very cute when you are frustrated. For many years you have always been very busy with work and family, but you always had time for me. You took your time to talk to me, really talk to me – not in a rushed manner, no, but like a loving son and friend. You took your time to explain to me again and again, how to turn on the TV – because I just couldn't remember. Your time, your precious time is in the box. (*Tap box*)

"You always showed how much you loved me by OFFERING to drive me to the dollar stores and the fabric shops that I loved so much. You even OFFERED to let me use you as a model when I was making that pretty dress for Maria, because . . . you are both the same size. And we laughed so much when you saw yourself in the mirror in that purple frilly dress with your hairy legs . . . you looked like your sister. The way you loved me – is in the box. (*Tap box*)

"Even when you were a little boy, and I broke my foot dancing salsa with your father – cause he cannot dance. You CARED for me night and day. And last year, when I could no longer take care of myself, you had me come live with you. (*Loud and emphatic*) I am the Mother! I am supposed to take care of my child (*Pause*) (*lower voice*) but now you take CARE of me. The way you cared for me is in the box. (*Tap box*)

"So you see my son, this box is not empty, those are just a few of the many ways you have made my life special. I placed in here, so I do not forget them. I want you to have them, so please keep it closed until later . . . when I am gone. Then when you think of me, look in the box and see what a special MAN you are. I am proud and honoured that you are my son – my little boy!"

Little boy! (*Act funny with body*)

Mom lost her battle with Alzheimer's and is no longer with us – but her box still sits by my nightstand. And yes I do peer into HER box from time to time, and it does remind me of the many ways I loved her . . . *(thoughtful)* It also reminds me how important it is to love others as well. It's funny, some see an empty box, but I see a box filled with special moments, intimate conversations, loving memories, and a blessing to my life.

Do you have a box??? One filled with memories of someone that has touched your heart in a special way? Have you touched someone's heart, and a box exists for you? We have all loved and been loved, but where do we keep those special moments? Mom chose a box. So have I. I now have a box, it's my box, one filled with moments of how MY heart has been touched . . . and soon, very soon, I will look my son in his eyes and say . . . *(extend hands out like holding a box)*"Toma" for you!

## BIOGRAPHY: OMAR RIVAS

Omar J. Rivas is an award-winning speaker and presentation coach, with 25 years of executive experience in Business Development, Sales, Marketing, Management, Team Building and Executive Level Negotiations. In 2010, Omar travelled to Palm Desert, CA. to compete in the World Championship of Public Speaking semifinals, becoming one of the World's Top 27 Speakers for Toastmasters International. The following year, Omar competed again and also made it as a finalist, placing him in one of the top nine speakers in the Toastmasters world.

For more information and to contact Omar, visit http://www.omarrivas.com

***Listen to *The Box* in the 7 Minute Champions audio***

# Say, Believe, and Do

## Winning speech by Granard McClendon

### 2011 District 43 (Jackson, Mississippi) International Speech Champion

I am better today in every way. I am better today in every way. You may ask, "why are you repeating that statement over and over?" Well, I am so glad you ask. I have discovered the three keys to success or being a winner in life: they are what you **say**, **believe** and **do**.

Let's start with **say**. I believe you got to say something to create something. See, before anything ever came forth, there was nothing, but God spoke words and created this very universe. Great leaders spoke words that created change in this very nation, such as Dr. Martin Luther King, with the "I Have A Dream" speech, and many are living that dream today. John F. Kennedy said "ask not what your country can do for you, ask what you can do for your country." There were other great leaders that spoke powerful words that not only affected this nation, but nations around the globe. But I had to ask myself, "What words have I been speaking to change my very world? Have I been saying I can, I can't, it's possible or impossible?"

## Believe

If the mind can conceive it and you dare to believe it, you can achieve it. Mohammed Ali was the greatest boxer on the planet, not just in his form, his speed, but in his mind. He believed he was the best. He even stated that to be a champion you must believe that you are the best; if you're not, pretend that you are! R. Kelly, singer-songwriter, said "I believe I can fly." I had to ask myself, "What am I believing?" Whatever you believe, it is not impossible.

## Do

Eleanor Roosevelt stated: "You must do the things you think you cannot do." Nike said: "Just do it." Doing it begins with getting away from everybody, getting in front of the mirror and asking oneself: "What do I want to do more than anything else in the world?" I want to share with you a story about two brothers that went to medical school together. By the way, they were twins: they came out of the same womb at the same time, lived in the same house, and had the same opportunities.

During medical school, right before graduating from medical school, one of the brothers decided to quit, give up. This brother became nearly homeless and stood on the street corner begging for change. Some days he would stand there and watch his brother drive to his successful medical clinic. One day there was a traffic jam, so he walked to his brother's car, knocked on the window and said, "Brother, I'm really proud of you. I heard of the great things that you are doing in the medical community. You are smart, creative, and doing great things." The doctor did not know what to say. He was in tears, but he looked at his brother and said, "The only difference between you and me is I am doing it and you are not." See, there is nothing to it, but to have a dream, vision, and "just do it". So I am better today and every way because I **say** it, **believe** it, and **do** it.

---

### BIOGRAPHY: GRANARD McCLENDON

Granard McClendon is a motivational speaker and life coach and an internationally travelled artist and musician. Granard rises to national prominence through his belief that God has blessed everyone with the tools to become a "Winner4Life", and as such, believes that persistence and determination, aligned with true passion, is the breeding ground for success. Through his high-energy message, Granard speaks to all who are desperate for a change of life, believing that one of the greatest things you can do in life is to do the great things that you were designed to do.

You can find and contact Granard through Facebook and Twitter (@G_McClendon).

***Listen to *Say, Believe, and Do* in the 7 Minute Champions audio***

---

# 7 MINUTE CHAMPIONS

## Listen to award-winning speeches from 7 speaking champions!

## Featuring speeches *from:*

- **Scott Pritchard**
- Lisa Panarello
- **Omar Rivas**
- Dhanashree Thangaraja
- **Phil Barth**
- Arnita Jones
- **Granard McClendon**

## Get your copy now –
## www.malachitalabi.com

# When Things Don't Go The Way You Want Them To . . .

## Winning Speech by Dhanashree Thangaraja

### 2011 District 35 (Wisconsin Milwaukee) International Speech Champion

Seven years ago, it was about the same time in the afternoon. I knew if I didn't hurry, I would be late for my 2:00 class. As I was walking down the hallway swiftly, I heard my roommate call out from the other end, "Dhana! Come quick!" I walked over to where she was. She was pale and struck with panic. I learned that Pavan, our good friend and classmate, had been taken to the city hospital that morning, where the doctors declared him dead already. A mob of emotions immediately flashed my mind. I remembered what a wonderful person Pavan was. I remembered what smartness, intelligence and talents he had. I remembered he could sing and play his guitar with such grace that sophomore girls would always be gathered around, asking him to play their favourite songs. I also remember wishing several times that I could be someone like him. I snapped back to the room when I heard my roommate shriek "Suicide! But, why?"

Two days later, when the University officials had conducted their investigation, we learned that Pavan had shared with one of his good friends how he wished his Professor would accept his research work more positively. He had wished that things would work out with his Professor the way he wanted. He regretted the way things were . . . so much . . . that . . . he chose to cross that line between living and not living.

Here was Pavan, very talented, smart and intelligent who was wishing that things would work out better, and here I was wishing I would be more like him, and the truth is: neither of us was happy.

Contest chair, judges, fellow Toastmasters and dear guests, have we all had moments when we wish things would work out in a way that we want them to? Whether that is resentment over the house we own or not own, or the 1998 Corolla car we drive, or maybe even living in cold Wisconsin against hot and sunny Las

Vegas! I have older friends who wish they had children of their own and others who wish they did not have children of their own. I have been hearing a lot of "could-a-would-a-should-a's".

I want to ask you, "When things don't go the way you want them to, what would you do?" All you fine people out there to my right and my left, what would you do when things don't go the way you want them to? If you do not have an answer or are still thinking about the answer, here are my two lessons for you this afternoon.

I have two cards with me; the first one is a Red Card.

## The Red card – Do not Regret

Martin Luther King Jr. said, "We should accept finite disappointment, but never lose infinite hope" – a powerful statement. Let's hear that again.

If you regret a decision that landed you where you are, and as a result of that, things did not work out the way you wanted, trust me. It's ok, and you know why it's ok? Because today if one door shuts, tomorrow there will be several doors that open for you. So lay aside the regret you have.

The second card is a Green card.

## Green card – Be grateful!

Have you heard of Arthur Ashe?

He was the only Afro-American male player to win the Wimbledon and two other Grand Slam titles. With a successful tennis career on his back, he used this success to confront several social and moral issues. However, he was diagnosed with a deadly disease right after a blood transfusion. He received a letter from a dismayed fan who had written, "Why did God have to select you for such a bad disease?" Ashe replied: "Listen, 50 million children around the world start playing tennis. 5 million learn to play tennis. 500,000 learn professional tennis. 50,000 come to the circuit. 5,000 reach The Grand Slam. 50 reach Wimbledon. Eight reach the Quarterfinal. Four go to the Semi-final. Two go to the Finals. When I was holding the Cup (*hold cup*) I never asked God: "Why me?" So why now, in pain, should I be asking Him, "Why me?"

Arthur Ashe is a great example of a person who felt immense gratitude in the midst of trouble. Are we being too busy today, planning what things we want, when we want things and the details of how we want things that we have forgotten to thank the Supreme Power for what we have? Are you thinking, "What do I have to be grateful about?" This instant, even as I am speaking, someone somewhere just left the world and their loved ones 'til the end of time, but you and I still have time. (*show watch*) Can we be grateful for that, but can we also be grateful because somewhere, this minute as I speak, there is a new life, and a new baby was just born. Life can be beautiful if we are grateful.

It does not matter whether it is a small or a big aspect, "be grateful" . . . always.

Ladies and gentlemen, it is true that we are all good people and we want the best for our family, ourselves and the country we live in. And despite our best effort, sometimes things don't go our way. But I want to tell you once more that when things don't go your way, "do not regret", but "be grateful".

The night after Pavan's funeral, I remember telling myself these lines from the Serenity Prayer that I had read a long time ago. "God grant me the serenity to accept the things I cannot change, the courage to change the things I can, and the wisdom to know the difference."

---

### BIOGRAPHY: DHANASHREE THANGARAJA

Dhanashree Thangaraja is an engineer by profession and a 2011 Toastmasters International World Championship of Public Speaking semi-finalist. You can find and contact Dhanashree through Facebook and LinkedIn.

***Listen to *When Things Don't Go The Way You Want Them To* . . . in the 7 Minute Champions audio***

# Everything Happens for a Reason

## Winning Speech by Arnita Jones

### 2011 District 8 (St. Louis, Missouri) International Speech Champion

Some people survived the earthquake in Haiti. Others lived to talk about Hurricane Katrina. Is it possible that everything happens for a reason?

Madam Contest Chair, Fellow Toastmasters and honoured guests. If you find yourself trying to figure out why you weren't selected for the job you knew you were qualified for, or why out of all of your siblings you ended up taking care of your cantankerous old father, or why no matter how many dates you've been on, you haven't found that special person . . . ? If you find yourself stuck or disappointed with life or questioning what possible good could come of some of the trials you find yourself facing, today I want to give you some ideas around why I believe we feel the need to hold onto this belief and share with you a story about a couple who found out just how important it is to know that fact.

We feel the need to believe in this well-known cliché because no one wants to believe, think or imagine that their life is a game of chance or a crap shoot. When you choose to believe everything happens for a reason:

- You feel stronger, because when you sense that everything has meaning, it gives you confidence.

- You feel wiser, because you see how everything connects. You see because "a" happened it led me to find "b" and then it allowed me to complete "c".

- You're more in touch with who you are because you know that you're living the life you were meant to lead. That your life isn't random.

Please don't misunderstand. Lots of things happen to us that challenge our sense of believing that everything happens for a reason. It can be anything. You get seriously ill at the worst possible moment. You think you've found the love of your life but something goes haywire between you and now the two of you are over.

You've had one of those really painful childhoods. You screw up and lose a lot of money. Someone you love dies.

I want to reassure you: when you discover the true meaning of the events in your life, everything changes. Take the story of Lucille and Leroy. They had been together for a couple of years when the decision was made to have a child together. Lucille already had a son by a previous relationship but Leroy had none. They tried to conceive a child and, after about a year of trying, decided to go to a doctor to check to ensure nothing was wrong. Now this was back in the early '70s, so there was no e-mail, text messages or instant messages, thus a letter was mailed to their home to inform them of their ability to have children. Lucille anxiously awaited the letter and, finally, after a couple weeks of waiting, the letters arrived.

Leroy was in the garage cleaning up their vehicles and Lucille opened both envelopes. The first one stated, "Dear Lucille, I am pleased to announce that you are perfectly healthy and can bear children." The second letter read, "Dear Leroy, I am sorry to inform you, but you are not able to have children, you are sterile." Lucille knew how desperately Leroy wanted children and decided to rip up the letters and throw them away and never tell Leroy what they actually said, but simply told him, "Honey, the doctor's report came in the mail today and we are both fine . . . I guess we just have to keep trying."

Months went by, and Lucille started feeling nauseous in the morning and throughout the day, and feeling tired and thought maybe something was wrong and went back to the same doctor who had tested them. Of course, the doctor, knowing that Leroy was sterile, told her she was stressed from dealing with work and family commitments and sent her home. The trend continued, and instead of getting better, the nauseous feeling worsened, especially first thing in the morning. She went back to the same doctor and was told that she had a tumour growing inside of her uterus and that is causing her to be ill. The doctor wrote her a prescription to shrink the tumour and sent her to the pharmacy. On the way to the pharmacy, the prescription flew out the window and, not wanting to take medicine anyway, Lucille decided not to get it filled.

Yet the feeling persisted; every morning she was nauseous and tired. Finally she decided to go to a different doctor and this doctor decided to do another test, a special test and told her he would call her when the results came in. A couple days later, the doctor called to tell Lucille she was pregnant. Ladies and gentlemen, I am here to tell you Lucille and Leroy are my mother and father. The question that has been stuck in my head for 38 years . . . had my mother told my father he was sterile, would I be here today? If my mother had filled the prescription and taken the pills to shrink the tumour that turned out to be a healthy 10lb, 10oz baby girl, would I have the mental capacity to share this story with you?

As odd as it sounds, it is true. Everything really does happen for a reason. It's taken me a long time, but I now see that even in some of the worst situations — and I've had my share of disasters — there are wonderful nuggets, hidden opportunities, and life altering lessons to learn. And somehow the universe knows we couldn't have gotten them any other way.

---

**BIOGRAPHY: ARNITA JONES**

Arnita is an up and coming public speaker, soon to be published author and a 2011 Toastmasters International World Championship of Public Speaking semi-finalist. She is a media-trained spokesperson for H&R Block where she has served as a District Manager for over 5 years. You can find and contact Arnita through Facebook and LinkedIn.

\*\*\*Listen to *Everything Happens for a Reason* in the 7 Minute Champions audio\*\*\*

---

# Sssssssss

## Winning Speech by Phil Barth

### 2011 World Champion of Public Speaking Finalist

The idea was big. It was bold. It was brilliant . . . but *(hold up right hand with index finger extended)* . . . Have you ever had a big, bold and brilliant idea? *(Pause)* Before you could taste success did you feel like something was holding you back? *(hold up right hand with index finger extended and pause)*.

Mr. Contest Chair, fellow Toastmasters, anyone who longs to taste success: the thing that holds us back is inside of us. Would you like to know what it is? It's a flock of chickens. Today you are going to decide that it's time to take out those chickens, get a pan, and fry 'em! SSSSSSSS.

*(walk to the audience's left . . . )* 23 years ago I sat in my cubicle at work. I had just met Beth. She was way out of my league. Back then I was a computer geek. Now I'm an Information Technology Geek. Back then, when it came to getting dates let's just say I wasn't the office George Clooney. I was more like the office George Costanza. *(Look back to the right)* still I thought "I want to ask her out."

As soon as I had that thought the relationship chicken entered the picture. "But what if she says no? Then you won't have a date."

"I haven't had a date in seven months!"

"But what if she laughs at you when you ask her out?"

"What if she says yes? What if we hit it off? Why 23 years from now we could be married with three kids and a dog."

"OR . . ." *(Step forward)* this is where these chickens get you. They build these elaborate Hindenberg comes crashing in to the Titanic disaster scenarios that will never happen, but they want them in your head to hold you back. *(step back)*

"OR . . . she could walk up and down the halls going, 'Phil Barth asked me out Phil Barth asked me out . . . Ooooh *(while vigorously flapping wings)*.'

23 years ago I had a flock of chickens that would darken my skies for days. Have you ever let something darken your skies for days? *(Pause)*

But that day in my cubicle I said "I'm going to analyse my life . . . with Microsoft Excel." I put together a spreadsheet and I calculated that at best I was given on this planet 32,867 days. I further had to deduct the number of days I had already spent on the planet, many of which were given to a chicken. I came up with a remainder of, no more than 25,309 ½ days. It was a half day because I finished the spreadsheet at noon.

I looked at that and said "That's all I have left!" How many days might you have left? Can you afford to give a single one to a chicken? I couldn't. I took that relationship chicken, I said *(Said while walking to the opposite side of the stage)* "Come on, we are going to her cubicle right now and we are going ask her out."

*(At Beth's cubicle put your elbow on the imaginary cubicle wall)* I got over to her cubicle . . . see I had my elbow on her cubicle wall because that looks cool. I know what you're thinking "Explains why it was seven months between dates."

I said "If you're not doing anything, Friday or Saturday . . ."

*(As chicken)* "Oh Friday or Saturday, she's going to have plans."

*(Pause and look back at the chicken, then back at Beth)* "If you don't have any plans. I was thinking that maybe we could go out to dinner."

*(As chicken)* "Oh go out to dinner? My goodness that's too formal. You should have said 'Get a bite to eat'".

*(Pause and look back at the chicken, then back at Beth)* "You know, get a bite to eat. You like to eat, don't you?"

*(As chicken, horrified)* "Oh great, you called her fat."

*(To the audience)* The relationship chicken had me on the ropes . . . Have you ever been on the ropes? *(pause).* When you're on the ropes you have to hold on to your big bold brilliant idea. I said "Maybe we go play tennis after work."

Mercifully she said, "Okay. Tennis. That sounds great."

I had a date. I walked around the corner and said (while doing a sort of victory dance) "I have a date".

I wasn't the only one with a date. The relationship chicken had a date. With the frying pan. Sssssss.

What is your big bold brilliant idea? *(pause)* What chicken is standing in your way? *(pause)* What chicken are you going to fry to make today and the next 25,309 ½ days better? *(walk back to the Beth side of the stage)* Because 23 years later, Beth is still out of my league. And we do have the dog, and we do have the three kids and we are married . . . to each other. I know what you're thinking and yes her name is now Beth Barth. That was a chicken she had to fry.

*(Walk back to the middle of the stage during laughter)*

But together we've been frying chickens for two decades now. And just this Sunday when I woke up I thought "I am so glad we fried the marriage chicken. SSSSSSS." And when our kids came in and served Beth her Mother's Day breakfast in bed I thought "I am so glad we fried the parenting chicken. SSSSSS." And later that when we headed to church and I sat down in the passenger seat of the car and I handed the keys to my 15½ year old son Kenny, I thought *(Fake crying)* "I've still got chickens to fry."

But that's why I'm still in my own personal fryers club. In fact, I've been frying so long I've achieved the rank of *(pause)* Colonel. I want each of you to be Colonel of your fryers club. Fry your chickens and achieve your Big, Bold Brilliant ideas . . . then taste your own success. Because, success . . . tastes like chicken.

## BIOGRAPHY: PHIL BARTH

Phil Barth has been in Toastmasters for 10 years. During that time, he has written speeches on topics as diverse as overcoming your fears, Project Management, and Winnie the Pooh. Out of more than 270,000 Toastmasters in 115 countries worldwide, Phil was one of nine finalists who vied for the World Championship of Public Speaking in 2011.

Phil has worked with non-profit organisations, manufacturing companies, and professional organisations. He uses humour with stories to produce programmes that yield results. Phil received his Bachelor's degree in Computer Science from Bowling Green State University, and his MBA from Xavier (Ohio) University. Phil is married with three sons and resides in Williamsburg Ohio.

For more information and to contact Phil, visit www.philbarthspeaks.com.

***Listen to *Sssssss* in the 7 Minute Champions audio***

# USEFUL RESOURCES

## Free online downloads

- 7 Secrets to Spectacular Speaking: http://7secrets.malachitalabi.com

- Learn from champion speakers: http://champions.malachitalabi.com

- Join the Champions' Corner for speaking tips and resources: http://resources.malachitalabi.com

## Books

- Using Stories and Humour (Essence of Public Speaking) – Joanna Slan

- The Power of Personal Storytelling – Jack Maguire

## Audio

The Edge of Their Seats Storytelling Home-Study Course for Speakers! – Craig Valentine

From Wishing to Winning! Making Your Speaking Dreams a Reality – Jim Key

## Speakers' websites

Maureen Burns Zappala — www.maureenz.com

Jim Key — www.jimkey.com

Craig Valentine — www.craigvalentine.com

Darren LaCroix — www.darrenlacroix.com

Made in the USA
Columbia, SC
16 November 2018